Personal Fulfillment *is* Success

Finding and keeping your natural edge

Joseph Seiler CPCC

Edge Press
Halifax, Nova Scotia, Canada

Published June 2003 by
Edge Press
17 Manchester Dr
Stillwater Lake, Nova Scotia
Canada B3Z 1G9

For further information please see
www.yournaturaledge.com/personalfulfillment

Editing: Paula Sarson, Lower Sackville NS
Cover design: ImageDesign, Bedford NS
Page design: Nancy Roberts Design, Dartmouth NS
Printed in Canada

National Library of Canada Cataloguing in Publication

Seiler, Joseph, 1950-
Personal fulfillment is success : finding and keeping your natural edge / Joseph Seiler.

Includes bibliographical references.
ISBN 0-9733135-0-1

1. Self-actualization (Psychology). I. Title.

BF637.S4S45 2003 158.1 C2003-903067-9

This book is dedicated to the magnificent people I have had the privilege of working with as personal coach.

Without you, I may never have uncovered and gained clarity about the truths that are offered in this book. Fully two-thirds of the content was derived in response to your requests for more information and deeper understanding. I have truly enjoyed developing this content and now again am privileged to share with those who read this book.

Thank you.

PREFACE

I have always been fascinated by how we operate, we humans. I noticed that even siblings with many similarities in their upbringing often didn't succeed equally, not even close, and wondered, "How come?" I experimented with ways to motivate and expand what a person was capable of and what they could get enthused about. I believe that I have some answers to my questions and want to share my observations about finding and keeping your Natural Edge. We all have our very own and powerful Natural Edge. Yet, far too many don't even know that, let alone step into it and use it to soar through life. Sadly, some people seem to miserably drag themselves through life.

My third career is in personal success coaching. I help people rediscover how magnificent they really are. Yes, all of us are magnificent. In my coaching work, clients often ask me to provide written support notes with explanations or suggestions for personal work to accelerate their learning. This book is an accumulation of those notes, so far, with some glue and bridges to make them into a more sensible read.

My underlying premise in writing this book is that the answer to your personal fulfillment is in you, not in me. The writing style may be unexpected. I have chosen to write primarily in the first person and present tense, especially in the personal introspection passages, so that the reader experiences the text as affirmation. The text speaks, whenever possible, with the reader's voice rather than with the author's voice.

When one reads about "you" noticing something or doing something or wondering about whatever, it is not the same experience as reading, "what am I noticing, what am I doing, I wonder about ..." The writing style in this book is designed to engage you in the process of finding and keeping your Natural Edge, to guide you through self-discovery using your own path, a path I do not presume to know. You have your own responses to the questions posed. Those responses show you what you need to know. Follow your intuition about the best path through the book, for you. And that will be perfect, for you.

Doing the right thing, for me, sets me free.
Doing anything else, even if it seems easier
in the moment, eventually bites me.

Question marks throughout the book are invitations to pause and learn something important about you. They are a gift to you. Consider yourself invited, hopefully even enticed, to mull over the material by engaging the questions. Reflect a few moments on each question before rushing onward to the next sentence. If you put pen to paper when reflecting upon the questions, then better still.

I wrote this book because I feel that I have an important message to share.

Welcome.

—Joseph Seiler

CONTENTS

Your Edgecode:

02D2-2ACB-03EB-BE18

INTRODUCTION

How to interact with this book

This book is meant to be experienced, not merely read. The format includes lots of space around the questioning sections to remind you

to take your time,

to pause,

to consider,

to "be with" the questions.

There is nothing extra for you if you finish the book in one sitting. There is, in fact, much lost. Thus, it is important to go at a pace that will allow a totally personal response to arise. That will likely mean setting the text aside for days at a time to ponder the questions posed or to derive the pictures that are suggested.

Something to ponder here is that *intention begets attention*. Then, that attention, in turn, begets action. Intent is the underlying fuel, the focusing lens, the highlighter that marshals consistent attention upon actions toward an objective. So …

What is my intent in proceeding with the experience of this book?

A Starter Sample

Responses to questions may pop into awareness that may seem, somehow, not right. Write them down, or at least notice them. Let the responses come as they may. There is no wrong answer. Allow the whole self to respond. Answering from the logical brain is valuable for sure, but it is incomplete. The whole body has intelligence beyond simple logic, and noticing *the sense response* of the body adds greatly to the real answers that we are looking for.

What is my reaction to this idea?

This question is the first sample. Pause now and notice any reaction to the idea of using the whole body to get answers to questions. Notice, too, that there is more than a black or white, yes or no, response. This is a different experience. Take a moment to "be with" this question. Notice the intellectual response and then open up to also notice the sense response, that tiny distant cousin of a thought, almost like a weak radio signal.

Ask, "What are the thoughts and also what are the feelings, what are the physical reactions, that I notice?" If the response is, "Hey, I don't notice anything," well, that may be. However, we are whole beings; our body chemistry and tactile sensory systems do respond just as surely as our brain responds. That twitch or that tightness or that soft overall feeling, is valid. That whisper of a word that just rolled across my mind is important. I may also sense fear, truth, annoyance, joy, all kinds of things.

The idea of body sensing answers to questions is the input. What is the response?

Again, take a moment to be with this question. Whatever little thing I notice is right. I cannot do this wrong.

Set the book aside and be with the question. Here it is again, awaiting a reaction.

> What is my reaction to responding to questions with my whole self?

What is to be done with those thoughts and observations? At this point, just noticing is plenty. Noticing that there does or does not seem to be a response that is wider than just an intellectual "answer" is plenty.

Well done.

Sprinkled throughout the book are suggestions for personal research work, like the example above. Responses to these can be written in the book. Personally, I find that less than satisfactory, so when I designed this book I added the ability to provide readers with an electronic copy of each question string and any tables or charts. That way you can use them on your computer, if you like, or you can print off as many clean copies, at any size, as suits you. Print off all of the material, or better still, just one string of questions, as desired, and toss them into the briefcase for consideration at lunch tomorrow. Whatever works.

Forms and Printed Aids

Each item of personal work is available in electronic format via the Internet on my web site. Simply log into www.yournaturaledge.com/personalfulfillment . Access to the site is controlled by a code, which is on the last page, just inside the back cover, of this book. Once on the site you can view the free content available to the public or click the *sign in* button, which leads to the *sign in* page for book owners only. The site holds electronic copies of all charts, question strings and personal work in this book along with some that do not appear in the text here. This way, you can have as many copies as needed and work either on screen or on hard copies. Answer directly on the site and answers are kept in your private folder, so you can build and interact with the material as you go and revisit anytime. Book owners also have access to new material, which is posted to the site from time to time and which is automatically emailed to you when first installed. The site access is provided for one year from date of original *sign in*. Lifetime access is available for a small one-time fee.

One Path

The path chosen to present the material is not the only path, just one path. The path begins with "Finding" (uncovering, surfacing, noticing) where/what I am right now. Then "Deciding" (discovering, celebrating, delighting in) what I really am, or could be, if I let go of, and/or replace, all of those ideas that I somehow accepted without actually personally choosing them. So, choose now. Deciding is the second step. Next come suggestions on how to keep those choices fresh and active. "Keeping" follows "Deciding." Finally, some generic and powerful support tools are provided in the "Tools" section. The information is reinforced with many examples and personal work suggestions.

The nexus of the material is in Finding and Deciding where personal work is offered in abundance. It is unlikely that anyone would do all of the work suggested. The idea is to offer you a number of options, from which you can engage the ones that feel attractive. Take a break once in a while. Graze around in the Tools section for a bit of variety and a more relaxing pace between the more intensive work pieces.

Since each personal work sequence is designed to stand on its own, you may find some minor repetition among them.

Reading and experiencing the book from front to back is just great. Scanning around, picking the areas that attract, is equally great.

DEFINITIONS

Natural Edge - that place in each of us where we achieve the "flow" of the Olympic athlete. I am doing what I am supposed to be doing and it is just *natural* for me. I am "in the zone."

Gremlin - a word coined by Richard D. Carson in his book, *Taming Your Gremlin: A Guide to Enjoying Yourself.* The gremlin is the internal critic that all of us have, the little voice that keeps us small, that tells us that we can't, that has a hard time accepting a compliment. The gremlin is the actor in the act that I put on for the world sometimes, when being my real self would be, somehow, too hard. The gremlin wants to keep me living in the guilt and worry of the past and the fear of the future based on the past, never in the present. Taming my gremlin is one of the most generous things I can do for myself. I recommend reading Carson's book more than once, plus sharing it with a friend. This is the simplest and easiest read that I have come across on this topic.

Another book that very nicely describes this internal critic is *Finding Your Own North Star* by Martha Beck. She refers to each person's Everybody. You know, "Everybody says …". Beck demonstrates how, once we investigate, Everybody usually turns out to be either one person or even just a perspective we have gleaned from TV or somewhere like that.

If you want even more, there is *Embracing Your Inner Critic* by Stone and Stone, which is a lively and in-depth treatment of the same subject. Lots of details and variants well explained. Also recommended.

Finally, there are a thousand ways to describe what Carson calls a gremlin. Check out *The Art of Possibility* by Zander and Zander, where they coin the term "the calculating self," or *A Course in Miracles* from the Foundation for Inner Peace, which uses the word "ego."

Be with - a phrase that means accepting yourself where you are and without judgment or analysis. Don't ask me to perform or act in any special way. Let me be where and what I am and accept me, as is. To be with a question is to let the effect of the query be felt and noticed in all of its forms – physical, mental, spiritual.

For instance, there are many little lies that we live with each day. The way I hold my stomach in when a pretty young lady passes by is an example. Some lies are bigger than that. What is it like to "be with" my own lies?

Inquiry - also called a fridge magnet or a bumper sticker. An inquiry is a question that is meant to leave the receiver curious about a matter that has been under discussion/investigation. The question is open-ended (not just a "yes" or "no"; requires introspection; may not have an answer at all) and is somehow engaging. The idea is to pose the inquiry again and again for many days; thus, the concept of the fridge magnet because I would see it each time I went to the fridge and seeing it would cause the inquiry to again arise for me.

Simply pose the question and then let a response arise from wherever. Notice the response and let it go by. Ask again, and again a response, and again let it roll past the consciousness. Make note of the intellectual and body responses mentally or on paper or not at all. Eventually, some responses will arise that surprise and educate and intrigue.

The nature of the inquiry is to bring up the inner, deeper, gremlin-free answers. The inquiry is to play with. Playing quiets the gremlin, as it does not appear that I am going to do anything but let the responses go by. By playing, I let the subconscious contribute directly as I gently, one by one, sweep away the usual and expected answers, getting, at long last, closer to the core of the matter. See also "Inquiry" in the "Keeping" section, page 107.

Namaste - I have heard the greeting "Namaste" ascribed to ancient peoples from Tibet to India to First Nations in both North and South America. It seems to be a word defining the universal relationship between beings. Namaste means, "I bow to the Divine within you, from the Divine within myself." When I offer it to you I acknowledge and honor our sameness.

FUNDAMENTALS

FUNDAMENTALS

Personal growth is about changing, becoming more in some dimension, advancing and growing better. What does "better" feel like? Some say better is having more control of one's life situation. Some speak of getting out from under and others tell us that it is doing more, yet doing it easily. Others speak of just "being" as the ultimate better way to live. If we explore the many manifestations of "better," one common and fundamental thread has to do with increased happiness, or to use another word, peacefulness. Our personal experiences of Yes! and Wow! and mmmmhhhh occur because what we have been doing is just so ... right and came together so perfectly and, it seems, effortlessly. Athletes call this state "being in flow." Elite athletes are able to achieve flow often. People, all of us, can lead elite lives and be "in flow," regardless of what we are doing.

Anyone who lives an elite life is more "*in flow*" than not. The very best seem to exist in some kind of higher state. Excellence is just their way. They are relaxed, natural and very present, with keen mind, bright, dancing eyes and totally comfortable, right where they are. They are not condescending or detached or odd, except in their freshness.

That is what "better" feels like.

How We Do

When we think of doing we think of action, results, manifesting, bringing forth. Doing is something usually associated with things accomplished by the body. How does the body do? It takes direction from the mind. The mind tells the body and the body does. How does the mind decide what it will have the body do?

There are two levels of direction given by the mind, the conscious and the subconscious.

We first learn to breathe, move and express ourselves. In our earliest years there is little capacity for self-actualization, spiritual fulfillment and the like. But over time those baser "things to do" are assimilated so deeply that we needn't lift them out of the subconscious to accomplish walking or talking or a thousand other rather complex tasks.

Overlaid on the basic physical and instinctual knowing of our being is our perception set about how the world works. Experience seems to be the driver for our uniqueness. All that I am is so much tied up in all that I have been. How I decide to act comes from my belief in how the world works. I derive more beliefs from interpreting my experiences. How I act is nearly defined by how I interpret my experiences. My reality matches my personally derived set of perceptions. Those could be scary, depending on what my interpretation of my experiences has been.

The conscious mind is the part of us that directs the variety in our days. The non-routine, non-automatic, "to do" list is generated consciously, as we go. We receive stimulus and give response. In order to deal with our world consciously, we need to absorb the stimulus, decide what to do about it, and then tell the body to implement our decision. Deepak Chopra calls this "place" where the decision is made "the gap." Many authors write about living consciously or living in the present moment. Mindfulness is to be wholly conscious.

Most people, most of the time, live on the fuzzy, misty border between conscious and subconscious. When we act primarily from the base physical, instinctual and perception base we are in that fuzzy place. Those who don't *ever* avail themselves of the conscious dimension are considered insane. We use words like detached, vacuous or out of touch to describe ourselves when the percentage of time in the nonconscious becomes rather larger than the norm.

But how does the conscious mind decide?

There are two "advisors" to the conscious mind: the ego (also called the gremlin) and the Spirit (also called the Self). The ego advisor speaks most quickly and most loudly and quite often tells the body to do things that reinforce our habits and that often backfire and bring us unhappiness. Yelling back when someone yells at me is a choice suggested by the ego. Those kinds of doing, like any, can become habits. Habits are automatic and are important deposits in our schedule of subconscious responses. The longer a habit is allowed to remain the harder it is to act differently. To act differently, even if I know it is for my betterment, feels foreign and unnatural.

The Spirit advisor, on the other hand, is patient and soft-spoken, which means that I have to resist the automatic response called for by the ego and be silent (in the gap) to listen carefully. Listening to the Spirit is like listening to our intuition, going with a gut feeling, going against the noisy and demanding ego. Ego likes to attack because it believes it can be hurt. Spirit knows it is completely invulnerable, and gently and simply suggests actions toward continued happiness and peace.

Interacting consciously with my environment has many advantages. I recommend it. But the conscious mind is not able to deal with dozens and dozens of directions for the body. The subconscious can, however, seemingly take care of a vast array of things to do, and all at the same time. The doing required to put oxygen into the bloodstream, to move a finger, to digest a Big Mac, to repair a cut, to yell back … Awesome, yet, so easy. Mindless? Sort of. Powerful? Absolutely.

So where are we? It seems that the part of the mind that we can interact with, the conscious, is the least powerful. The subconscious appears to be the powerhouse, yet it runs on automatic, or habits, most of which seem to arise from the quick, loud, attacking ego. So in order to "do" something really significantly different from how we did it before or to establish some new habit, we have to have the conscious mind train the subconscious mind. We may also have to first "untrain" the subconscious if we are removing an unwanted item from the historically embedded to-do list. David will have to rule Goliath. The minnow will have to eat the whale.

This can be done. I have been "doing" it since birth, maybe not purposely, but I have been doing it. But now I am questioning if all those automatic programs I have accumulated are what I really want. I have decided to take more control of myself. In order to do things differently (to effect a change), I must think differently.

I like the opening sentence in the first chapter of Napoleon Hill's book, *Think And Grow Rich*, which says,

> Truly, "thoughts are things," and powerful things at that, when they are mixed with definiteness of purpose, persistence, and a burning desire for their translation into riches, or other material objects.

A similarly provocative quote, attributed to Norman Cousins, is:

> A human being fashions his consequences as surely as he fashions his goods or his dwelling. Nothing that he says, thinks or does is without consequences.
>
> Just as there is no loss of basic energy in the universe, so no thought or action is without its effects, present or ultimate, seen or unseen, felt or unfelt. Every single thought that I have has a consequence.

If I want a new behavior to "stick," to become automatic, to be implemented by the seemingly infinite capacity of the subconscious, I need to use the conscious to develop and then enter (assimilate) the desired program. But this time it will be done while fully aware, on purpose.

About Finding

We live in a world that tells us everything of worth is "out there." Knowledge, material things, relationships, forgiveness, affirmation and more appear to come from outside of us. In this kind of existence, defining myself, who or what I am, relies on indicators outside of me. When I describe me I tend to use descriptors that are designed to please the outside, to please others, and these are not always based on what I am really like. Further, I do not always pause to notice how I actually feel about those descriptors.

Somewhere within me is a knowing that some things are right and some are wrong, *for me.* These "knowings" are valuable to me. The ego competes with these knowings to drive my reactions. If I don't consciously know what is indeed very important to me I can find myself reacting strongly in some situation (from the automatic) and not really understanding why. If I can surface my personal core values, understand their origin and the power they have over my actions, I can better understand reactions and then introduce more chosen responses, instead of being the hapless passenger asking, "What just happened?"

Finding out more about who/what I am and noticing my reaction to that way of being brings clarity about what I am, reduces unexplained internal struggles. Getting real clear about me (Finding) lets me more consciously choose toward my fulfillment. Self-forgiveness and permission to be myself both get easier. Stress melts.

About Deciding

Until this moment, I have somehow chosen/decided my way through life. When I better understand the choices I have made, the ones I haven't made and the results that I am experiencing, I can then more purposely design more of what/who I am. Uncovering how I got to here allows me the opportunity to use the same methods, now recognized and understood, to move myself to interact another way with the world – a more consciously chosen way. I come to a place, a new place, of choice in the design of my own life.

Wow. I actually get to decide.

About Keeping

Having decided, the matter then becomes making the new into the normal, for me. I got here by reinforcing beliefs and acting repeatedly and consistently, for various reasons. Now I do the same to take me toward my greater fulfillment in full awareness of my conscious reason.

About Permission

When I am stuck on an issue, part of the reason I am stuck is that I am using the same approach, over and over and over. I build a rut and make it deeper with each attempt to move on. Ruts are singular ways of seeing things, ways of doing things, ways of being that are based on habit or what Steven Covey calls paradigms in *Seven Habits of Highly Effective People.* When I come to an issue and feel stuck, I need a new approach, something to bounce me out of the rut.

Typical reactions may include questions like:

> Why is this happening again?
> Why can't I get past this?

These questions tend to take me to analysis and logic – usually what got me into the rut in the first place – making the rut deeper as they are a rehash of the whole darn thing, yet again. And they tend to generate a feeling of accusation. Not really very empowering.

A more powerful approach is with questions like:

> What about this happening again can help me?
> What do I notice that might get me past this?

This more open form of question tends to help me explore around the issue, instead of staying in the same place, only deepening the rut.

To open my mind to ways out of the rut, I need to get unstuck. It can be very enlightening to ask questions like:

> What permission do I need to give myself in order to blast me past this?

When that type of question is asked the mind notices the odd request. Just posing it can jolt me out of my rut. "What do you mean give myself permission?" The question really asks, "How am I contributing to being stuck?" It challenges the idea that the source of the issue is outside of me. The question challenges me to take some responsibility for where I am and how I am feeling. It asks me to "look wide" at the matter; looking wide is not possible if I am in a rut. Framing the question thus honors me in that it anticipates *that I actually do know* what to do, that *I can* blast past this. It brings me to the present moment and allows me to choose again.

Solutions are not in the ruts. Once I have bounced myself out of the rut I can see further afield. By taking some responsibility I also retake some of the power that I lost when I entered into the rut. That feeling of hopelessness is diminished. I regain both control and power. That is what makes the "permission" questions so powerful. Allow me to illustrate with a personal example.

> I was having a great deal of difficulty communicating with someone connected to a committee that I served on. I understood this person was responsible for an important part of our group effort. As time went on, the work that he was to do was not getting done, and my efforts to communicate were a consistent failure. Things were becoming critical with regard to this person's responsibility, and I felt increasingly frustrated. I had tried everything. He didn't respond to emails or return phone calls. It had been many weeks.
>
> I had dug my rut, that is, my approach to the problem, very deep. I moved to questions like, "What could I do to break the impasse?" Answers I came up with like, send a registered letter and get legal advice, were really poor options in dealing with a member of a volunteer committee. At the eleventh hour of the project a colleague posed the questions, "What permission do you need to give yourself about communicating with him?" and "What permission do you need to give him in this situation?" My answers were to give me permission to stop my insistence that he communicate with me on my terms and I gave him permission to possibly not even know that he had this responsibility.
>
> Boom went the bubble of frustration. Zoom came an elegant solution to it all. The things that had been holding me in the rut had evaporated. I began to consider, what if he didn't even know that he was supposed to do this stuff? What if he were so busy with work commitments that his secretary had strict orders to say no to all volunteer

> matters? Perhaps the communication with my fellow committee member was not exactly what he thought it was and so on and so on. The permission questions broke the deadlock.

The journey you are about to undertake with this book needs your permission to go a different way, to experience anew, to move on and into a new place with fewer ruts. Giving permission is a way to get to the place of creating. Yes, get that pencil moving and give yourself permission to write answers to the following. You have begun!

What permission do I need to give myself …

- at home?
- in my extended family?
- in my career?
- about my significant other?
- in the way I ask for things?
- in the way I receive things?
- in the way I talk to myself when I screw up?
- in the way I talk to myself when I do well?
- etc.

What permission do I need to give myself in order to fully experience this book?

FINDING

FINDING

My Present Reality

I often act without thinking all that much. I also often think without thinking all that much. My thoughts are often based on assumptions, past expectations and habits. I run on automatic a lot of the time. What if some of the reasons that I developed those assumptions and expectations (which formed into habits) are not really what I initially thought they were, or what if they have changed since I first encountered them? Oops.

In order to find the answers to these questions I need to stop and observe what I have been doing. I need to find out what my values appear to be compared to what I seem to believe that they are. I need to bring my awareness onto my self to find out what I am like. Otherwise, how can I express to anyone, even to myself, the description of the place that is my Natural Edge?

What would it be like to make my habitual self indistinguishable from my true Self? To be someone who is present and not simply running on automatic, every action a well thought out choice? People who do that are pretty awesome. They seem to have an edge, maybe "the" edge.

"Finding," this section, is about clarifying where I am today. What am I right now? What works and what doesn't? What are the disconnects from my true Self? I'm going to explore to learn more.

Observing Ourselves

A wonderfully simple way to begin the process of "finding" is to observe ourselves. We are not usually taught to observe ourselves. There is something delightfully liberating about assuming observer status. The viewpoint of the observer seems to have less emotion and less attachment. It is an easy viewpoint to adopt and to enjoy.

In her book, *Elegant Choices, Healing Choices,* Marsha Sinetar tells us that we unconsciously observe ourselves all the time. Further, she tells us that we punish and reward ourselves based upon our observations about our choices in life. Hmmm?

When I observe, in the now, when I just notice, consciously, I gain more clarity about what is actually happening. In this place of greater clarity there are fewer assumptions and there is more truth. Thus, the automatic and judging part of me loses potency. This gives me an enticing freedom to choose with greater confidence rather than to react automatically. I like to feel good. When I choose well, I feel good. When I choose from the perspective of the observer, I more often choose well.

The key here is to *just notice*. That word "just" reminds me to do nothing other than notice. No evaluation of any kind is invited into the act of just noticing. By just noticing an event and my reaction to it, I am outside of it, as the reader of the story is outside of the story.

The information gained in the noticing is given to the observer. The observer, who resides in the relative calm of the skybox rather than in the thick of the game, can then explore for meaning by gently, slowly, calmly looking at what has been noticed, looking from every angle. If I *relax into the observer role* I am more objective than in any other view that I might adopt. As the key to noticing is to just notice, the key to observing is to allow even the weirdest, most impossible angles to arise and fall away in my mind. I cannot discover something new if I only allow the old, the familiar, the safe into my awareness.

Gently, I let it all in. I play.

> Example: As the observer, I might have the following sequence of exploring questions arise from a thought that I noticed:
>
> What if that unspeakable thought is partly true? *(Rather than getting hooked into the idea that I "shouldn't" have unspeakable thoughts, I just notice and go on.)*
>
> What does believing that thought is unspeakable do for me?
> *(I get curious and explore in one direction.)*
>
> What part of that thought isn't unspeakable at all?
> *(And I'm off in another direction.)*
>
> If someone else did what I observed myself doing what might the truth be?
> *(Detach further to gain even more objectivity; besides, I am playing so am allowed to go anywhere I like.)*

Noticing is a gentle art. Be gentle. Stay with the thought string and just notice it flow along. Get curious. Ask questions. Try new variations of the question. Play. But stay with the question.

> Another example: What am I like?
>
> Variants might include, what do I like? what is it like to be with me? what do others like about me? … and so on.

One more point. The observer may also receive interpretation suggestions from the gremlin. I can tell it is a gremlin-based thought if my reaction to the possibility is to get smaller, to restrict my options, to feel guilt or to feel urges to abject apology and other angles that tend to just beat me up. If I find myself picking up gremlinesque static I am not just noticing, I am also judging. Give all possibilities equal, unattached observation. I allow the negative to be there but don't buy it, just notice it. Deciding can come later.

At this moment, I am observing myself typing this manuscript. I notice that a part of me is concerned with getting this message to you with absolute clarity. That part of me is a bit nervous. Another part of me is scanning my life experiences and conjuring up the next bit of text. Still another part is laughing at me, observing me telling you about observing. I am here, in the present moment, observing me being me – somewhat comical.

There is information about me in my choice of the word "concerned." What is that really? It could well be my gremlin not wanting to make a mistake, trying to impress you, wondering who would read this anyway, or still something else. I could also interpret that much more harshly and take myself down an unhappy road that would threaten the completion of this book. If I stay with this analysis I am not "just noticing" but have shifted to interpretation. That will soon enough take me to judgment.

Instead, I choose to return to just noticing and stay as the observer. As the observer, the "I don't want to make a mistake" and "I want to impress you" and "who would read this anyway," are just noticed and let pass. I am allowed to laugh out loud at some of the things that arise. I am, after all, having fun.

The observer is a present-moment persona that is always at choice. As the observer, I am able to notice, and then decide, later, what to do. Later, in these cases, is but a fraction of a second. I act upon due consideration of a larger base of true information, rather than react on automatic from a base of assumptions from the past.

How can I be more the observer and less the automaton? That question is the same as, "How can I change a deeply ingrained habit?" Breaking habits takes conscious effort. After all, it was consistent repetition that generated the automatic responses that I am now noticing. Noticing, just noticing, and letting the thoughts pass without acting on the usual automatic response is the key to being the observer. Unattached observation allows all angles to be considered. Among those many angles is information from which to choose my actions. By letting the thoughts arise and fade, without judging or responding, insights from heretofore-suppressed angles can arise.

Some ways to notice more often:

- Set my watch to beep on the hour and use that reminder to notice.
- Place a yellow sticky-note on my doorjamb at eye level as a reminder.
- Put my watch on so I read it upside down.
- Move a ring to another finger.
- Put a tiny rock in my shoe.
- Put something unexpected and noticeable in my pocket.
- Take something that is usually there out of my pocket.
- Put a marble in my sock by my ankle.
- Put on a toe ring.
- Put my watch on the other wrist.
- Place a piece of dental floss between two teeth for a day.
- Move something to a new place on my desk.
- Take a different route to work.
- Use the other hand to hold the phone.
- Get a loudly ticking clock for my desk.

The idea is to bring my awareness back to the present and into noticing. To observe and to choose my actions I need to be present-minded, rather than absentminded. Techniques like the above will capture my attention because they create disconnects from the expected and automatic way that the world has been established for me, until now. The disruption reminds me. Most of these will work for a few days before they too become expected. That's when I change to another disruption. I keep disrupting and noticing until noticing, being the observer, becomes automatic.

What happens when I interact with a colleague in the observer role? It might be something like:

> I notice my automatic reaction begin and I let the urge pass. I notice what is actually true and real here, at this moment, and only then do I decide, choose a response and then act.
>
> Notice, right now, what am I sensing at my right kneecap. I use my whole sensory system and just notice. What is happening there as I adjust my posture? How is that kneecap feeling? Move my leg and notice some more. Which sensors am I using to sense this kneecap? Stay with it for a few more seconds by slowly re-reading these few questions and just noticing (or maybe "knowticing").
>
> Note that thoughts about the past and future have been temporarily set aside. What has it been like to do that?

Ultimately, the observer idea applies to any situation. I observe myself interacting with another person. I notice the level of emotion and the thoughts that flash across my mind as I chat with this person. What is happening in my body as this person communicates with me and the tempo and tone and topic move around? What is happening with me? What are my automatic response favorites? What assumptions do I usually like to bring to meetings with this person or that?

> I try this with the first person I find to chat with.
> I notice.

When I interact with a question, I do so from the viewpoint of the observer. So doing allows me to engage the question more fully rather than simply letting it, and my response to it, both slide by. Receiving a question with the observer viewpoint lets me fully engage it. A richer, deeper response is therefore possible.

Writing Down an Observation

It can be very powerful to write from the viewpoint of the observer. I learn more about me. What was my last experience of noticing myself like? I write that down in detail. I note all the experiential parts of that noticing. What was my body chemistry doing? How fast was my heart beating? How was I breathing? How much was I sweating? What was I feeling? What weird thoughts seemed to ramble across my mind as I was doing this? What was the biggest surprise? What was the "oh-oh"?

This is an opportunity to notice but not to measure, compare or judge. Just notice. It is an act of Acceptance, Acceptance of Self. That is an act of the Self.

Given the tool of the observer viewpoint, I can now better start to notice where I am as I begin my journey of change. Let me engage the following questions as observer. Let each question arise and have its answer arise behind it. Then again the same sequence with a variant that may arise. Let the question arise, the answer, a variant, another answer, another variant, and so on, until it feels done. Then go to the next question and engage that question in the same conscious way:

What am I like?

When do I lose it?

When do I get sad?

What behaviors are really working for me?

What behaviors are sabotaging me?

So, what has it been like to be the observer with these five questions? What do I now know?

When noticing provides a sliver of knowing, I call it knowticing.

I can therefore ask, "What am I noticing?" or graduate to "What am I knowticing?" The results are usually different. Knowticing often shows me an undeniable truth. To ask, "What am I knowticing?" is like asking, "What is actually true here?" and getting an answer from an inner well of knowing.

Some say that the installation of a new habit takes at least twenty-one days. The habit of noticing and being the observer is not the norm for most people. Attending to development of the new habit will take effort and time. Readers will be invited to use the observer viewpoint often in the rest of the book, so the habit will get built, if you let it.

What Am I Really?

Some will say, "I finally saw the real Jane today when she said ____." Or maybe, "John really lost it today." What is the "it" that he lost? It's as if they *slipped* and accidentally revealed a previously hidden truth.

If I somehow keep track of my actions for a day or a week or a year, what will I learn about me? How much of the time am I working hard at bending the assumptions of others? Better still, how much of the time am I working hard at bending, or hiding, the beliefs I have formed about myself? Euuhhh, that is a tough one.

What core values do I exhibit through my actions? Is the "it" that John lost the facade that covers his true self? How much energy am I putting into being what I am "supposed" to be? In other words, how much energy am I putting into supporting values that aren't really mine?

Have I ever caught myself saying something like, "What was that I just said? Or did? That is not like me. Where did that come from?" It came from somewhere in me, how is it possible that I don't seem to know from where?

Why not just be myself? Great idea. But what if I don't exactly know what I am about? What if people won't like the real me?

What if I got to know and like the real me enough so that I could then act out my truth, all the time?

For the moment, imagine that I do know my Self. I have a pretty solid idea of what my ideal, true Self is. Given that I can describe my Self, I can then start to program my subconscious to make choices in my interactions with life in a way that reinforces and demonstrates my Self. I do that by consciously choosing my actions and acting consistently for a sufficient period of time so that programming sticks.

When does unconscious action happen? When is the programming inconsistent with my Self? When I react and emotions are high, those inconsistencies can show up. When I lose "it." When I am not thinking but just running on automatic. The gremlin is in charge then. That is when unconscious actions happen.

The programming of the auto response (that was learned and memorized by the subconscious) needs to be addressed. I programmed it, so I can change the program. Re-programming is about reclaiming choice in my actions.

Hmmmm? Is it possible that I sometimes choose poorly? Of course. I am human and therefore fallible. The programming of the subconscious is a process of accepting, and acting on, a string of consistent choices. Consistency is the key to programming. So an occasional slip does not program (or "unprogram"). I may not choose my actions consciously; therefore, what gets programmed in is the trend or general pattern that is evident in my actions. If I don't choose to notice, and from that void then mindlessly act, the pattern is likely a mishmash of behavior adopted from my surroundings. I am trying to fit in, so I act like the group, with the result that I program myself with values that I might not wholly embrace if I consciously chose.

The same logic could work in reverse, if I am trying *not* to fit in. Because my criteria for choosing action could be extreme and become "any action that demonstrates that I do not fit in," I could again end up acting in a way that I might not wholly embrace when I review. I have acted from other than conscious choice. Having programmed myself, I act (react) according to those unconsciously programmed values that aren't really mine.

I struggle to define my true Self. "Taking back my life" means taking it back from this place of relative mindlessness in having haplessly programmed myself. The journey to taking back my life means delving deeply into my values, the ones I can really own, providing the solid basis for my personal fulfillment choices.

Values

We are taught to hide our magnificence. Yet it is in us and cannot be denied. There is something in me that is true and "that something" knows what is right and knows my calling, knows why I exist. Uncovering that knowing is the big exhale, the ultimate stress reliever, heaven on earth, salvation. When I am in my calling I am invulnerable, whole and magnificent. My inner sense of what is right is an expression of my core values. Uncovering those core values is essential to understanding what I stand for and to finding and keeping my Natural Edge.

When I live out my values I feel complete and in harmony. When I don't, I feel unfulfilled and dissonant. Values are reflected in my way of being. They are not things to be bought or stored. I cannot be other than right with my values if I am at peace. It can be uncomfortable to uphold my values sometimes. I may have to confront someone or do something that is truly hard. Yet, once I have acted and done the hard thing, I feel right. A sense of integrity and a knowing that I did what was right for me replaces any discomfort. When I sell out on my values, the disquiet can last for years. In the first instance, the discomfort is likely a fear and in the second it is a growing guilt or remorse over having let myself down.

Decisions based on my highest values always provide the most satisfactory result. Always. Thus, the following sections and personal work around values is the essential foundation to attaining greater personal fulfillment.

What is a value?

My thesaurus lists the following: principles, morals, ideals, standards, ethics, beliefs, mores, what's important. Yes, that's it. A value is what's important – to me. I believe in honesty. So when I notice that the change the store clerk gave me includes ten dollars too much, I speak up and give the extra money back. I believe in justice, and believing that the store owner has withheld salary from someone unjustly, I hold onto the ten dollars then give it to the person who was violated. I believe in serendipity and the wisdom of the universe so accept the ten dollars as a gift coming to me for a worthy reason, yet to be revealed. What is happening here?

My values are the basis upon which I decide what to do when I am presented with a potential moral dilemma. So a value is a pointer to what I, just me, believe with absolute conviction and independently of what others think. It is that deep-down right-versus-wrong calculator.

When I am struggling with what to do, it is usually an indicator that two or more values are facing off on the issue at hand. It is not black and white. Whether honesty is my highest value or justice or the serendipitous wisdom of the universe makes a difference in what I do when presented with a surprise ten dollars at the store checkout. When the decision I take leaves me with a residue-free feeling of peace, I have chosen from my core values and honored the highest value among them.

Personal core values are just that, personal. I have mine and you have yours and there is no requirement that we agree on which value is highest. In society, the most commonly accepted and shared values become the law of the land. We value human life or liberty or equality or rights to protection under the law, for instance. Even here there are people who do not, for themselves, value these above other values. These people, when they act on their values might act against the law and find themselves in trouble. This is not a plea for conformity but an observation that we are somewhat different in our adoption of core personal values. Values, per se, are not right or wrong, but they are the basis upon which I decide, for me, what is right or wrong.

Where do values come from?

One source of values is the authority figures that we encounter as we enter and grow into our place in the world. Moralistic statements, firmly and convincingly made by one who is larger, older and more powerful than I can have a deep impact when I am four or nine or thirteen. Values adopted in this way are often adopted for survival. The consequences of arguing against the moralizing figure don't look attractive.

Trying on another's values is a way, sometimes a good way, to answer a question that I have about how the world works and what is right and wrong. We adopt and refine values using this method throughout our lives. It is the dominant method when I am very young, but remains a source even for a mature adult. I notice that so-and-so does this or that and gets appealing results, so I will do likewise, seeking similar results. That can work. The only issue here is the level of maturity from which I make my observation and choice.

The maturity factor is large here. A fifteen-year-old may not fully appreciate the differences evident in the choices around a given situation compared with the wisdom that a forty-year-old might bring to it. Peer pressure is a major contributor, providing not only models but also a push towards them. Societal pressure is a close cousin to peer pressure, so it is a contributor to our values fabric throughout our lives. I observe and choose what I think will work for me.

Another important source is the process of values clarification. This is taking the choosing beyond the simple carte-blanche adoption of whatever it takes to fit in. The clarification process is one of adopting, testing and noticing and then adjusting and again testing and noticing.

I am somehow convinced that honesty is one of my highest values. How do I react in the store checkout when presented with an extra ten dollars in my change? What if I don't notice the error until I am at home? What if I don't notice until the next day? Or if I am on a trip and don't notice until I have driven a number of hours away from that town? What if I owe ten dollars to a very nasty person who has just seen me and is heading my way at the very moment that I notice the extra money? If in some of these scenarios I would go back and in some I wouldn't, what does that mean about my value of honesty? What happens when I reach the "cutoff" beyond which I don't go back? What other value has been proven higher at that point?

This method is not for the very young, and it is not a casual inquiry in any event. Clarification of values is a journey into the Self. The process of clarification is ongoing.

Which values do I own?

I thought I valued honesty, but there comes a point where there is no way that I would do all that would be necessary to get the ten dollars back to the store (even if I learned that the clerk making minimum wage may have to pay it back or may lose her job?). Whoops. What just happened? Another value may have just shown up and now we have the makings of a moral dilemma. Becoming the observer when presented with a moral dilemma is a great way to get in better touch with my core personal values.

The only values I really own are the ones that I consciously test and then choose freely as mine.

That is almost enough. I then need to act on my values and to act on them consistently. Yes, in public. And having acted consistently in support of those values, I can notice my feelings and notice the residue-free feeling of peace. I just "know" this is the right thing to do (for me) and that is, in the end, the only real reason I do it. Those actions are based on the values that I indeed own.

Values and Gremlins

Acknowledging and honoring values is the best way to overcome a gremlin, the ever-critical and uncomplimentary creature that sits on my shoulder and tells me that I am small and unable. The gremlin is the source of doubt and inferiority. The gremlin will argue against almost any decision I make in the incident with the extra ten dollars and the store clerk. Gremlins cannot be reasoned with.

Values are like a huge spotlight pointed at the gremlin. The gremlin can't stand to be exposed so it shrinks back. There is a certain unarguable rightness about acting in accordance with my true inner values.

Why Values Are Important

Values-based decision-making allows me to stop defending what I choose because I know, truly know, why this is the most important and right decision for me. "For me" is the part that frees me from blindly conforming to the group. Conformity can also be a value, but if I have higher values around a particular issue, it is easy for me to go my own way when necessary and feel just fine about it. I am solid in a way that gets noticed when I am "on value," when I just know what is right, *for me*.

My values are evident in what I do and what I am. I can begin to uncover my values by assessing *what I am* day by day. What I say and what I want may give some indications of my values, but *what I do* really tells the story. Thus, in order to search out core values I review my life experiences. What have I actually done? What do others say I have actually done?

What was the value that drove me to make one choice in a particular circumstance and not in another situation?

What are the values that have not been honored to cause me to hold these stones in my stomach over certain past events? What value did not get honored there?

Really want to get me going? Trample on my values. That has been known to start wars. The highest motivations are those that call people forward to honor their core values (peace, liberty and justice, etc). Goals set in accordance with core values are most likely to be achieved because the incentive is built in. Vision and mission are most compelling when values are embedded in them. Values are to die for.

However, what you will die for I may not care about at all. We may differ in what we value, but we are the same in that we respond most strongly to our own values.

When I determine that a change is needed, is it not that a value is crying out to be honored? When I say, "That's it, no more," a suppressed value is calling out for acknowledgment. Values are the foundation of personal peace and values not honored are the seed of discontent.

Through Affirmation to Fulfillment

What I do is a manifestation of my values. In order to stay on track with my values I need to act consistently in accordance with them. Thus, once I have uncovered what I believe my values are, and through experimentation learn what they actually are, I can *program in* the appropriate behavior by acting consciously. One vital component of programming the mind to act automatically in a certain way is to "affirm" the desired behavior. The affirmation is a statement expressed in the first-person present tense, declaring what I am. I am honest. I am clean. I am physically fit.

Because my absorbed values come to me from many sources, some of them dubious, it is quite normal to learn after a values clarification sequence that I am not exactly acting in accordance with a certain value. I said I am honest, but after the clarification sequence above, well, I am not so sure about just where in the list that value sits. An affirmation is most powerful when a core value is supported.

Note: The material from here to the end of this section is intense work. Be gentle. Take time outs, but stay with it, as the result is the basis for everything to follow. Enjoy.

Uncovering My Values

Mining for values is a process of uncovering what I am, what I am like, what I consistently do. There are four *values exploration* options in the following sequence plus two more on the web site. I visit them all and then engage any one or more of them that attract me. I can return at any time to do some more, for they can be very powerful. Next are the four *deepening explorations* that support, refine and enhance whichever combination of the values explorations that I decide to experience. (All six of them make a valid combination too.)

Values Exploration 1
Question Strings

As responses to the questions arise, check what other words define the particular value, in order to define the word as it uniquely relates to me. I make written notes as I enjoy the following question strings. (Adapted from *Co-Active Coaching* by Whitworth/Kinsey-House/Sandahl)

What must I have in my life in order to be fulfilled?
- What would I have if I had these?
- What would having these give me?
- What, then, would be possible for me with these in hand?

What are the underlying values in these must-haves?
- What would I instantly stand up for?
- What would I fight for?
- What would I die for?

What do I obsess over?
- What would my colleagues answer to that?
- What are others "supposed to" know better about me?
- What are the things that must be done right, always?

Think about a peak experience.
- What was the high in that experience?
- What part of that high would I want to have again and again?
- What is valuable to me about the high in that peak experience?

What about an experience that is opposite to peak, a total low?
- What was the low in that experience?
- What part decimated me?
- What upset me so about that particular part?
- (If I flip to the positive side of the lows, I get the value impugned.) What value got trampled there?

What in my life do I truly have handled, the things I always do the right way, for me?
- What habits do I cherish?
- What would others say I do all the time?
- What would I miss most if I were not allowed to do it again?

What really upsets me, my hot buttons?
- What am I quick to react to?

- What would I instantly stand up against?
- What would I fight against?

When am I most alive, natural and at peace?
- What is happening when I am perfectly OK with the world?
- What do I notice that attracts me as nirvana?
- What are people like in the perfect world?

What is the most important problem to be solved in the world today?
- What else needs to be solved with that?
- If those were solved, what would be happening that isn't now?
- What is it about that something else happening that has juice in it for me, that grabs me?

What can I let pass as simply someone else's opinion but that I know is true, in another way, for me?
- What is undeniably true, no matter what others say?
- What is so obviously true that there is no need to even defend it?

Values Exploration 2
Reflecting Through the Hedge

Pen and paper ready. Take the viewpoint of the observer. Enjoy.

> I imagine that I am walking in a lovely garden with many paths and flower beds and hedges. I round a corner and hear my name spoken by a group of people on the other side of a tall hedge. They are describing me and what I stand for. What do I most want them to be saying? What do I want them to have recognized about how I show up in life?

> Now peek through the hedge and notice that the group includes some friends and colleagues and neighbors and people who I knew in the past, even some older people who knew me as a child. What do I truly want them to be saying about what I stand for?
>
> Look again. In the group are a few people who have not liked me much and some with whom I have even had run-ins. Somehow I know that the discussion in the group is about the truth. What do I feel these people, who may not particularly like me, must acknowledge about what I stand for, if they are going to tell the truth? What will they admit that I stand for?
>
> And wait, someone has something to add. They forgot to tell about one more thing that is undeniably true about what I stand for. What are they saying?

What do I notice about me now?

Values Exploration 3
Immutable Me

I have looked a little bit into my past to discover where this or that value originated. It is sometimes also helpful to go into the future to design my perfect Self, by choosing to enhance certain values. In this personal work, adapted from *I Could Do Anything* by Barbara Sher, I look back and forward through my life, identifying what was, is and will be significant along the way.

For the ages between five and ninety-five, at five-year intervals, I fill in the table. I just write the first thing that comes to mind rather than struggle to find the "right" answer. The first thing to mind is about as right as it gets. I don't need to make this a big deal; it is, in fact, better if I don't. This is play.

Note: Copies of this worksheet can be printed from this book's website, www.yournaturaledge.com/personalfulfillment , using the unique access code on the last page of this book. Also see page 3.

AGE	MAJOR EVENT	WHAT I LEARNED	THE MOST AMAZING THING I SAW
5			
10			
15			
20			
25			
30			
35			
40			
45			

more...

AGE	MAJOR EVENT	WHAT I LEARNED	THE MOST AMAZING THING I SAW
50			
55			
60			
65			
70			
75			
80			
85			
90			
95			

After I review the whole table, I write a paragraph entitled, "What I Would Like to Tell Young People," from the overall view that I have at age ninety-nine. Write the paragraph now.

Also, upon completion of the paragraph, and from the viewpoint of the observer, I think about:

> What were the values present at each step along the way?
>
> Where did they come from?
>
> Do I still want to keep them or change them or discard them?
>
> What are the values represented in the future list and what has caused me to put them there?
>
> What is the attraction?
>
> Which of these have been heretofore-ignored values?
>
> What are these items that I have put into my future?

Finally, I write the sentence or phrase or word that says, "This is the immutable me." The phrase is something to remember, the one really important thing that I want to bring to mind if I ever feel unsure or am being pressured or in any way just don't know what to do. This immutable me will ground me at the place that is truly important to me, regardless of what others think. It is inviolate, and when I listen to it I am totally grounded. The immutable me aligns with my purpose or calling in life. It really feels like home, to me.

Examples of immutable me statements:

- I always have enough time to do what is right.
- I am a teacher.
- I lead.
- I need very little.
- I can wait until any storm passes.

The exercise is particularly valuable because it draws on my past and projects into the future. Notice the things that defined me when I was very young and later just naïve and, of course, my aspirations for the next decades. Look for the threads in the final table that could define me if someone else read it without me there to amplify it and say, "Oh no, I didn't mean that." I adjust it for clarity.

I take a deserved rest for a day or two.

Welcome back.

Now review the table again, a little bit differently.

I am an investigative reporter doing a history project on the person who filled in the table (me), and I am trying to uncover what was really important to that person. Of course, I presume they did mean what they wrote, just as they wrote it. Whatever comes to mind about "that" person I write it down (even if I think it is wrong about me). If a number of possibilities arise, I write them all down. I am on a quest. I include every possibility. I am relaxed. I cannot do this wrong.

And then I ask:

What were the values present?

Which ones seem ambiguous?

Which ones are not at all what I had in mind for myself?

Which ones do I want to adopt/keep, change, discard or enhance?

What do I now recognize about the values represented in the future list?

What do I now recognize about what caused me to put those values there?

Approaching these questions from the position of investigative reporter gives me the objectivity to see more about myself. These questions are the nexus of uncovering my apparent values to find the ones I truly want and then decide to own. If I have derived a value from my personal experience and analysis of what works for me, and if I consistently act on that value, then I own it. It becomes mine. The way I am, how I am, is wholly and naturally intertwined with that value. When I act contrary to that value, I feel as if I have eaten a piece of watermelon rind. The above sequence is about noticing the values that I *seem* to own and then consciously deciding whether or not I want to keep them.

I stay with this for a while, as long as I want.

Values Exploration 4A
In the Flow Noticing

The following is an exploration that will help surface my values. What answers arise as I gently, thoughtfully read through the listings? I observe. I see myself floating as a unique molecule belonging with, and welcomed by, the other molecules, doing my part, being my Self, in the stream of life. This could take about an hour; it's a slow, steady stream.

I exhale.

I relax.

I open up to the questions with sincere and gentle curiosity.

I give myself the gift of time on this one.

In the stream of life, slowly sensing myself as I ask, what is my experience of …

Gently flowing in the main body of water. *I am now keenly aware of my connection to the rest of humankind. What is that like? What am I typically doing while here?*

Roaring over the falls. *What is an example of when that experience is exhilarating and another example when it is desperately frightening? How are the differences observable in my body reactions?*

Swirling playfully among the pools and rocks. *I lose track of time and just forget my cares. What is my experience in one of these times?*

Going backwards in an eddy. *No matter what I try, it is backwards I go. What is the feeling like and where do I most notice it? Which part of my body speaks the loudest in these situations? What's funny about these situations?*

Being at the bottom of a still side pool. *Sometimes I like to just sit and watch the rest of the world do whatever it does and I like to be still, when I don't need to compete at all. It suits me to do little. When I am here my experience is like … The thing I need most in these times is …*

Rolling in the slipstream around a fast bend. *Woo hooo! There are days when not much gets in my way. It's all like butter and I am a hot knife. My energy is high and my intuition is spot on. I zoom and that feeling shows up in me as …*

Moving safely and quickly enough in the mainstream. *Life is good, the world is round, and the speed of it all is just fine, thanks. What is my body chemistry like in these situations? What are my thoughts like? What's unique to these moments?*

Unable to see around the next bend. *Describe a time when this is an adventure and another time when this is severely unwelcome. What is happening inside of me at these two times?*

Repeatedly slapping into a rock. *Again? "Why is this happening," seems to be the question of the moment. What is my reality at these times? What really works well at these times?*

Unable to get out of the stream. *I must and have to and should and can't. What are these like? What does my body have to say about these? What is my typical reaction?*

Just being with the other water molecules, whatever we are doing. *It all seems so right; everything is good. I belong here and it is just nice to be here. What is this like for me? What is possible from here?*

Being swallowed by an animal. *Being trampled, overtaken and not valued. It happens. When it does, what is my first reaction? What is my second reaction? What is really happening here?*

Floating happily in the sun and whistling quietly to myself. *Not a care in the world. I'm with myself and enjoying my company, yet present to the rest of the world, if it cares to join me in this pleasant place. I don't need to join, but others can come along with me, if they want to. What are these moments like for me? What is my typical thought pattern like in these times? What is my overriding emotion?*

Escaping the crowd to join the mist for a while. *I'm just not as keen as always to play the game today, and I do have things I would like to do. So nothing rude, just focused on what interests me today, thanks. What is my dominant body chemistry here? What am I actually doing when I am doing this?*

I step out of the stream to take a closer look …

So, *what am I like?*

Where do I show up big for myself?
Where do I sell myself short?

What's it like being *the way* I am?
What's it like being *what* I am?

What's missing?

What's oh so beautiful?

Now look back to see what values are represented in each of the responses. Interesting.

Values Exploration 4B

Exploration 4B, an extended version of 4A, includes other examples of life situations to help surface values. Please visit www.yournaturaledge.com/personalfulfillment .

Values Exploration 5
Notice Decide Commit

This web-based exploration uses an approach that causes me to:

1. Notice my actions around this situation/question.
2. Notice the core values that I say I hold high.
3. Notice any inconsistencies between my actions and declared values.
4. Decide if there is a program that I want to change.
5. Finally, consciously commit to change that program.

Please visit www.yournaturaledge.com/personalfulfillment for the complete exploration and experience.

Explorations Wrap-Up

Note the values that I hold in all of the responses that I made to the set(s) of explorations that I decided to undertake. Upon completion of the values exploration set(s), pause here to consider a few questions.

Having completed one or more of the values explorations …

What is new now?

What is the scariest item that has arisen?

Which one of these will I have the hardest time explaining to my closest confidante?

What changes am I now considering?

What change(s) am I ready to commit to?

On a scale of one to ten, how strong is each of the commitments I just made?

What do I need to do in order to get the help I need to meet these commitments?

Understanding My Values

Values become most visible when I am confronted with an issue, when something intrudes into my complacency. When a choice gets my attention, I am usually choosing between values. Inconsistency in life upsets my view of the world and my value system of beliefs. Ultimately, my value system is a decision tool. It is the measuring stick I use to help me decide/choose. I develop my measuring stick over time, and it changes as my understanding of what is true, *for me,* evolves.

The ego/gremlin wants to take over in this arena and wants me to choose toward protecting it. To do that I would need to believe that getting smaller and safer and holding back (never try something new or speak up or …) is my true path in life and that my fulfillment is there. My true Self is infinite and invulnerable. It knows that it's important sound can wait to be added to creation or that it can speak anytime and be welcomed; it matters not. Thus, the Self and the gremlin/ego are in direct competition.

Thing is, the Self could care less, because it is infinite, invulnerable and has all the time there is, and beyond. Self knows that it is not at all threatened. It is a competition with only one competitor, one who must fabricate the adversary. So the gremlin/ego fabricates opinions that suggest I must protect myself.

How can I better understand my values? A schematic rendering of my value system evolving might go like this:

> If ten is absolutely most important to me, where is "control" on my values list?
>
> "It is probably an eight, maybe more."
>
> What is more important than control?
>
> "Health is more important."
>
> And what is more important than health?
>
> "Peace of mind is even more important."
>
> Where is control getting in the way of my peace of mind?
>
> "Why can't I have both?"
>
> What is getting in the way of my having both?
>
> What does peace of mind look like?
>
> What's happening when I have it?
>
> What's absent when I have it?
>
> Where are Self and ego in this discussion?
>
> What needs to change?

And so my values, my measuring sticks, are always changing – not without struggle. They can change toward my Self or go the other way. It is fundamental to know that I am changing, experience by experience, and, at my core, it is my values that I am adjusting, testing and evolving. The trick is to choose freely from among the alternatives, to be with the options and to go toward the Self. Anybody watching me will know what I truly value by noticing my actions. What am I prepared to speak up, stand up, fight, or even die for?

Deepening Explorations 1
Processing and Deepening Values

The last few pages have offered personal work to help uncover candidates that could be my own values. Next I just take note of the answers that arise as I gently, thoughtfully read through my listings. I see myself as an observer would. I see myself as a small but valuable part of humanity, doing my part in my unique way.

Naming a value in a single word is a starting point in fleshing out what is my true value. I can say that I value honesty. Does that include telling someone their outfit is horrid when they seem to believe it is lovely? A good start in clarifying my values is to string the definition – I add three or more words to "honesty" to help clarify what form of honesty is my highest value and to distinguish it from my other strings of words around that same root.

> Honesty/true to self/totally present with others/ being myself

> Honesty/fairness/telling the truth/a full day's work for pay/don't steal

These two strings start the same, but the respective full pictures of the value are different. Stringing my values in this way gives me a bit of texture and flavor. It helps to show up the ingredients of the value that I am espousing in my own way. It is like saying, "We are having stew for supper," compared to saying, "We are having curried chicken and carrot stew simmered in goat's milk for supper."

Now I return to the list of candidate values that I have surfaced and, from the observer point of view, I "string" them.

Having done all of that, having developed every value into strings, what can I now say about what I am, what I am like, what I consistently do?

Deepening Explorations 2
Seeing Values in the Context of My Life

Another useful way to get better hold of my values is to seek out where in my life a particular value arises. I need to check the "doing" parts of my life to ascertain what the flavor and texture of this value might be. For the values identified so far ...

> What is it about this value that is so important?
>
> When I support/uphold this value, what is happening around me?
>
> When was the last time I noticed, really noticed, this value in my activity?
>
> Where else in my life does this value show up?
>
> What are three other words for this value?
>
> What is the feeling in my body when I let this value slide?
>
> What is it like when I am totally honoring this value?

Where did I get this value?

What is still valid about that source, for me, today?
What's *not* still valid about that source,
for me, today?

What else is at least as important, to me,
as this value?

What is a better name for this value?

I am gentle with myself and let this work take the time it needs to put a light on my core personal values. This is a good time to, again, set the book aside and return after a generous assimilation break. Maybe do one value per day. There is no rush.

Values-based living

I assert that when I am truly living my core personal values the world is my oyster. I live in a kind of peace others might not even understand, but they wish they could have it too. I "know" what is right for me and am able to say either yes or no and to sincerely mean it, without any kind of guilt or second-guessing or gremlin interference. Ahhhh, where all work is play and there is always enough time, because I know what is most important to me.

Deepening Explorations 3
Grouping Values

I have done a lot of work in exploring who and what I am. Now I need to get all that valuable information into one spot to examine what I have and move to the next step. I am ready to write and I am ready to put some quality time into the following questions. These are the fruits of my labor, so far, answering the big question, "What seems to be important to me?"

Now I list, in related groups, all the values that surfaced in the personal work sessions up to now into the following categories:

- Notice, maybe complain a little, when this value is impugned, but do little else.

- Notice and think about this value quite a bit, maybe speak up when it's impugned or add support when it's honored.

- Definitely speak up and vote publicly about this value.

- Stand up and be counted as strongly for or against. Be an advocate for this value.

- Fight for this value. Something has to be done and I am willing to do it, or at least help in a big way.

- Go to jail for this value, if that will help, or make a very big deal over this until something changes (quit my job, fire my partner, etc.).

- Fight to the death for this value, if need be.

I am worth putting some time into this listing. I let it be honest to a fault. If it crosses my mind I put it down somewhere. No thought is wasted. Now I have a bit of hierarchy within my values. I am seeing, possibly for the first time, what is actually important to me. I may also have learned that some of those things that I thought were important values, actually aren't very important after all. Wow.

Deepening Explorations 4
Meeting My Own Values

Entering observer mode …

Which values have I discovered that I probably didn't choose myself?

Which values do I sense a bit of mistrust toward?

What are the values that I seem to be giving short shrift to? These values somehow got on the list but I let other "priorities" set these aside quite regularly. Which ones fit that mold?

What others might be added here?

What is the gremlin saying about some of the changes that have crossed my mind as I have gone through this section? List the candidates for change, even the smallest ones, and put the gremlin comments beside them all.

Want to crank up the intensity? Add a column that lists the first three steps to making the change. Now listen to the gremlin holler, and write those utterings down too.

Review the answers to questions asked up to now.

Which ones am I proud of?

Which ones am I not proud of?
(Gremlin in action again.)

Which answers can I notice some physical reaction to, however small?

What is the pattern there?

Roll these bits of insight into the already developed listings and explore a little further.

What am I noticing about the connections between the various value explorations?

What pattern is arising?

What can I now say about me,

the new,

refreshed

and clearer me?

I exhale. Breathe. Just let it sit for a day or two. I revisit to add, adjust, embellish, but not to delete. Or maybe none of that. This is a picture of me. It's all important and all-important.

What have I learned about my Self?

Congratulations. Only a few make it through this work. You are worth the effort. Congratulations indeed.

Now rest a bit. Let all that has been experienced just sink in for a few days before continuing.

DECIDING

DECIDING

What I Really Am

The previous section, "Finding," helped me to find out more about who and what I actually am. It also pointed out sources of my decisions to be this way or that way and helped to somewhat prioritize my most important values.

In this section, "Deciding," we focus on describing our best and future Selves, climbing inside a fleshed-out image of *whom we choose to become*, stepping fully into who we actually are.

What do I choose to change?
What values do I choose to adopt?

Candidates for Change

With caring towards myself and gentleness in the magnitude of changes chosen, what have I decided to change? What is my list of candidates for change?

Ten items might be too many. Two is likely not enough. Since these are only candidates at this point, I jot down any possibility that comes to mind. I don't concern myself about whether a candidate for change is a bona fide value; they will all be derived from values. When I look at this new list, I notice my reaction as I slowly and fully consider each of these possible changes using the following investigative sequence, *repeating for each candidate for change.*

What am I thinking?
What am I feeling?
What's happening in my body?
What is my emotional state?

I just notice and make a note. No evaluation.

What is the source of the little voice that is asking for, or maybe even demanding, this change?

Is that me or someone else speaking?

Who really wants this one?

What is the source of the little voice that is urging, or maybe even insisting, that this change *not* happen?

Is that me or someone else speaking?

Who would also have to change if I made this change?

What is the motivation for placing this change on the candidate list?

What is the deeper consideration here?

What will be different for me if I make this change? What will be different for others?

Who are those others?

How will things be different for them?

What is the payoff for making this change?

What's it worth to me?

Specifically, what would the level of payoff need to be in order for me to actually make this change?

What is the loss if I make this change?

What do I have to give up?

Who will object if I make this change?

What is valid about their objections?

What parts are not valid?

How does this candidate for change align with my career?

What is so important about this candidate for change? What is the value being honored here?

Whom am I going to impress with this change?

What do I notice about that?

Am I supposed to say "just me"? What if I didn't say that?

What is the happy, wonderful, yahoo part of changing this candidate?

> On a scale of one to ten, with ten as absolute ecstasy, just how happy a yahoo is it?

I take my time. This is not a race and there is no deadline. Each candidate for change deserves my full consideration through the whole investigative sequence.

As I go through the introspection for *each* change candidate, I start to become attuned to the ramifications of that change. I notice the fear of trying something new and the grieving over losing the old habit. It is all here, within me. Now, having noticed myself interact with the candidate list of changes, which one(s) still, after introspection, call to me as needed and indeed welcome changes? I am gentle with myself and keep this list short.

I come into observer mode. I choose.

The candidates have been culled. My intention is now upon a few select changes that I know will give me more of what I want in life and/or less of what I don't want. I know that these few are worth the effort to put into effect.

Now I set the list aside. I set the book aside. I let the whole thing sit a day or two.

Visualization

How does someone perform who has achieved the change that I seek? "Seeing" that performance image in an experientially rich manner is called forward memory visualization.

It seems that when we experience in advance the result we want, it somehow sets up the future so that the path to the desired result is made easier. I call this kind of experience "advance memory." It suggests that the thing we are experiencing in advance is already there, as if this thing that we want we in a way already have. The result then becomes, somehow, more something that we are now allowed to have, rather than a never-to-be-attained pipe dream. The practice of creating advance memories strongly supports the "realistic" requirement of a successful affirmation. (See "Affirming" page 115.) This practice is also the foundation of visualization.

A powerful and effective visualization gives the subconscious mind a target to pursue. I need to choose the visualization as an advance memory, as something that I already have, and the subconscious will then put its infinite power and creativity to work to get it for me (kind of).

Does well-developed visualization produce what we call coincidence?

Some will say there are no coincidences. Suppose I am seeing what I have decided to see.

> *What if coincidence is only the first time that something I am looking for (asking for) is noticed?*

A coincidence usually shows me something that I am pleasantly surprised to notice. What is that telling me? What if I sometimes "ask" subconsciously?

Some say there are no coincidences. What do I say?

Detailing the Visualization

I like visualizations that are detail-rich, with lots of trivial embellishments. So if I am creating an advance memory of the state of my business, I include things like the following:

I can smell the fresh vinyl in the new cube van that we own.

I laugh out loud as I reprimand an employee when he accidentally bumps the van with a long piece of wood that he is loading for a big job.

The crew are smiling and chuckling and busily doing, doing, doing.

The work schedule board is bigger than the one we used to have and it is clearly full; someone drew a happy face in the corner.

The sun is shining.

The big potted plant needs watering.

It is nearly 2:00 PM and I am only now going to lunch with my wife; I am hungry and feeling a satisfied kind of tired, having accomplished a great deal since arriving at work this morning. She is very happy too.

One of the employees brought their dog to the shop today; what a treat!

Two of the guys said thank-you this morning for the new health plan that was implemented last week.

My desk is semi-tidy, yet organized with a near-empty in-basket and an almost checked-off to-do list on the side wing.

That bookcase is still overflowing with whatever. I will some day have time to organize a small fire.

There are four outgoing proposals in the mail basket for pickup; I know we are front-runners on all of them. We will certainly win at least three of those. If we lose any it will be because the community is starting to see us as too dominant, and they are giving some NewCo a chance. What a great new challenge.

> The award for most improved company in the industrial park is hanging near the doorway by the water cooler.
>
> We finally have a janitor to help us with all the handyman work and general cleaning. The shop guys really appreciate not having to do that work anymore and the new fellow seems to really like doing it. What a win.

In reading through these statements I get a picture of what it is like in the future and a bevy of questions surface. Some statements may seem irrelevant, like what is that about a dog? Well, what would have to be happening for me to be so happy to see an employee's dog on the plant site? What is my mood? What is the employee feeling like? What are the employee-management relations like? Is this an extension of my laughing when the employee hits the brand-new van with a board? Is this a believable scene? Isn't something being said, something positive, in the comment about the plant needing water? Would I like to be a part of this company? Which of my values are supported in this scene?

Lots of details and on the other hand not many details. This is "holding loosely." Rather than specify bank balances and staff numbers I concentrate on the feel of the new business scene and on how success enhances that scene. This way is more experiential than visualizing numbers. I am going to lunch at 2:00 PM and it sounds like it may be a leisurely affair at that. I see consistent indicators of success as I want it to look for me, and I believe it is just great, for me.

I can include numbers if that is what helps me to experience the advance memory. So I make the experience the kind that raises *feelings* for me. Advance memory anchored in experience is all-powerful.

Note also that the values I have surfaced as most important to me and the changes that I worked so hard to decide upon are embodied in the experiential picture. This visualization is of the place where I am fulfilled, living my values, having accomplished my desired changes. I have arrived. I have found my Natural Edge.

In her book, *Creative Visualization,* Shakti Gawain suggests that successful implementation of visualization includes four important parts:

> Set a goal.
> Create a clear picture of the outcome.
> Focus on it often, from a relaxed, open state.
> Give it positive energy through affirmations (see "Affirming," page 115).

One could add,

> ... and then stop trying to force it. Let it come.

Gawain goes on to test for three necessary elements:

> Desire – Do I really want what I say I want?
> Belief – Do I really believe that this goal is possible for me?
> Acceptance – When what I want shows up, am I ready to take it?

If I answer the questions in the three elements above with an undeniable yes and the four (or five) important parts are in place, I can start getting ready for the goal to be achieved and clear a space for it in my life. It will come and sooner than I think.

Visualization is a superset of affirmation. Visualization means generating the picture of the desired outcome. Affirmation is the speaking of having already achieved the result.

The purpose of visualization in the process of finding and keeping my Natural Edge is to evolve the end point of the plan, the objective, the goal. "Evolve" because it is usually an iterative, or a getting ever closer, process.

After creating a scene something like the one in the example above, I ask a truckload of questions to clarify and elicit details of all kinds, to test for reality, to recognize embodiment of my own values and to deepen the image in any way that I can.

I write the visualization and rewrite it without looking at the first version. I do that as many times as I can stand it. As I do this over a period of weeks, I watch the picture move and grow and become reality. That is the objective, to make the picture true enough and detailed enough that I believe it can be mine, and that I can easily recognize it when it shows up for me. When I have a visualization of the state of things five years from now sitting in my conscious mind, it is extremely easy to draw a contrast to what is in fact real for me today. That contrast can generate a meaningful to-do list, a plan to get me where I want to go. It is easier to make a plan when I know where I am going.

Finally, it is a phenomenal decision aid to check today's decision, whatever it is, against the five-year picture and to ask, "What is the decision that will get me to that five-year picture sooner?" Start the habit of doing this and "five years" will arrive in half that time or even sooner.

Five- and Two-Year Plans

I may not exactly know where I want to be in two or five years. But what if I could design my future by describing where I would like to be? There are lots of books and even scientific studies that support the idea of designing our future. Try it and see.

The choice of two and five years is deliberate. I use the visualization technique and write the five-year scene first because it is far enough away that it is believable that every barrier, small or large, between what I really want and what I have today, could realistically be gone. So I write with confidence that it just might be possible. I write experientially, with lots of sensations – how I feel and what it smells like and the colors of everything and the mood in the room and the sounds I hear and what I'm wearing and how those clothes actually feel on my body, everything. I write about what I'm doing and what others around me are doing and the energy in the scene and the laughter and what I had for lunch that day and what others are saying around me and to me and about me and what the papers have written about it all. I visit the places that are intriguing for me, which may include my home or my bank account balance or my office at work or the car I am now driving or how I am interacting with people. Wherever my imagination goes, I just follow and describe it fully. This picture is big and detailed and I am having fun with it. This is an experience in my *advance memory* rather than past memory.

My advance memory is not just a big wish list. That would be just a wish list. This is a picture of what I can actually see as my future in five years. My insight in this matter is astoundingly good. I let the picture flow out and just note the details so that I would recognize it if it showed up in front of me. If I have a question about part of the future, I simply "go look." The answer comes. I'm not concerned with "how" questions that may arise as I paint this picture. "How" questions tend to elicit all the barriers. I stick with the "what." I just paint the picture of the desired result, drawing on my whole Self, not just my brain. I allow heartfelt intuition to play here.

I might want to revisit this visualization, and add, adjust, embellish, dream. But I resist deleting. That item was important to me when I wrote it. I'll leave it there.

How much is enough? That is totally up to me. I cannot fail. There is no minimum and no gold star for extra pages. But I make sure to let this process run its course in order to capture every facet of my advance memory. I allow myself to empty the whole vision into the writing. I will know when that has happened.

If I don't like to write, I can forget the fancy prose. I can use words and phrases, enough so that I can evoke my vision by reviewing what I wrote. Sentences are not required. Drawings are just fine. Capitals and correct spelling are not required.

What is required for this visualization is that I experience the future, five years from now, and do so in a way that I can share and talk about that experience later.

Enjoyable.

When I am emptied of the five-year visualization, I let it sit for a few days and then, without looking at the five-year description, I write a similar piece for just two years from now.

Same idea. I allow the things that I don't expect to be gone by then to stay present in that two-years-from-now description. Keep things real. This picture is a little more from my head, but I still let the experiential part flow as best I can. It is typical that the two-year picture is more quickly and easily completed than the picture for five years. Again, I do not let reality, my reality as I see it, be lost. This is not a wish list where I just forget to write some of the facts as I know they will likely be in two years. I let the reality remain in the description and let it coexist with the dream part. A big wish list is just … And a lie about reality is just …

I set that aside for a few days.

Now I write a parallel description about today. "Parallel" meaning that I address the same topics as I did in the two- and five-year writing in order to describe where I am today. The contrast is what I am seeking here. Cryptic and quick are the hallmarks of this last little document. I just jot down the present picture, as honestly as I dare. I only need deal with the items already named in the two future plans for those are the ones I seem to want to change.

Derive Measurements

How will I know that I am done? What will it be like when I have accomplished the desired change? What markers can I ask an objective outsider to watch for that will hail the accomplishment of the desired changes?

My first visualization example was a great beginning. Now I go to that visualization, go to the five- and two-year plans and quantify, quantify, quantify everything.

I view the end point holistically. If I see a certain level of success in my career does that include having a dog or other pet? Is the sun still up when I return home most days? What is happening in my stomach as I view myself in the workplace at 10:00 AM and at 3:00 PM and at 5:30 PM? As I notice those advance experiences, what else is around me in the workplace? If I work in an office, for instance, what does it look like outside my window and what is in my in-basket and what does my calendar look like and what types of questions do people typically ask me and when was the last time I laughed? What is the feeling like at home and what are people saying and doing there? What is my advance experience when I imagine meeting my romantic partner, my family, my neighbors? What is the state of my bank account and what are the amenities I see around my physical environment?

I am specific, yes, but if I hold the vision too tightly, I don't allow the universe to innovate and bring me what I ask for most quickly. I stay with outcomes. What will be happening when I have achieved the goal? "The big plant needs water."

For instance, "I know at least four of my neighbors by name and have had at least two of them over for a meal" is loosely held, yet kind of specific. Someone could easily test to see if I had achieved that goal or not, while at the same time it tells me what needs to be in place for my experience to be what I desire it to be. So what is the definition of neighbor here, or do we care? That plant that needed water in the visualization section, what does that tell me? Are we so busy that no one had time to water it? If so, define busy in a quantifiable way. Something like "X percent of staff hours logged are against valid, paying jobs," is tightly held. Too busy to water the plant but not so busy that an employee can't bring a dog to the shop for the day. Yes, that's it. That is a loosely held outcome. So, in this place, what is the average monthly profit? That is a number, but a number backed up by a whole picture of experience. The number says nothing about the dog and at the same time now says everything about the dog. If I am a numbers person I use numbers to measure eventually. At this point I go for the feelings in the experience of that plant needing water and seeing the employee's dog.

Holding More Tightly

OK, now it is time to use numbers and to hold the outcomes more tightly. What are my measures? How will I know that I am "there"? What will that feel like? What is the advance memory and what are the measures in my picture of that advance memory? Split out each statement from the visualization that I have developed and even statement fragments, where sensible, placing those on the left side of the sheet. Then identify and write down the measurable indicator of "proof," the more tightly held kind, on the right side of the sheet. I do this whole piece of work in the future vision of myself. I go to my future place and bring back the data to write down. I inhabit the future visualization. If I don't know the answer to a question, I simply go to the visualization, walk around inside that picture and get the answer.

I can have fun with this, but I'd better be firm in identifying a measure. If it seems elusive, I put down what is happening around me at the time and investigate that for measurables. I find something to put into my mind, some sign to tell me that I have made it to my desired end point. I need to describe it well enough so that I will recognize it when it shows up.

Middle Chapter

One fun way to push past a blockage to writing a future vision is to write a fictitious chapter of a story. It is about me, five years from now. I accomplish fantastic feats with aplomb and panache. I have a new name that somehow reflects my biggest, most fantastic dreams for myself.

The other characters in this narrative are those whom I see as important to me five years from now. I might include a few new people whom I don't know yet. In order to generate this chapter I get the people I do know involved to help me in my imagination. I ask them what they are doing five years from now, how we interact and, most importantly, what they see me doing then. I have fun with this; I bring popcorn and let my imagination roll. The other characters get to have new names too.

It does not matter what I put into this chapter. It is a middle chapter, not the beginning or the end. So there is no need to be concerned about how the heck this or that character becomes as they are in this story. It is a middle chapter, so there is no need to reach a conclusion, to figure out how to make it end. It is fiction – totally free-form – so no need to be restricted in what might happen to these other characters. I am sure to capture what I am doing then, five years hence. I ask for details about situations that arise, what I am wearing, what the food is like, how much money I have in the bank, when was the last time we went skiing, etc. That the characters are actually the contributing speakers in the exercise keeps things grounded and it doesn't usually get too weird. But if it does, well, I let it go. No real harm here.

This middle chapter idea provides an easy-to-generate picture of me five years from now. I don't need to use every scrap of this input. Visualizing how others see me is just the gravy around the main course of *my* picture of myself. From the gravy, and my own heightened knowing of what I like and don't, I can generate a two-year interim picture that answers the questions about how I get there, still in story form. Call it an early chapter of the same story. From that comes the resulting decision aids to guide me in answering the questions, "What do I do now? What's next for me? What do I really want?" and so on.

I look at the story's events and decide what is realistic for me to actually accomplish. The parts I don't see myself doing are wonderful seeds for inquiry into "What would it take to ..." kind of growth questions. I can go e xploring with my good friend "what if ..." I also observe the story to notice the values represented there. Let me see what I can learn about me with this idea. I am curious.

I enjoy my Self five years into the future!

SMART Objectives

Having moved from visualization, to loosely held outcomes, to more tightly held outcomes, I am ready to make a plan. The plans most easily, or most likely to be, realized are clearly stated, written down, have a deadline.

These fundamentals are well covered in the SMART format. SMART is an acronym that stands for:

Specific – Clear enough that I can recognize it when I have it and so also could another person. There would be no argument, no hairsplitting.

Measurable – A black-and-white, yes-you-have-it or no-you-don't indicator.

Action – This is a result that I can see because of something happening, rather than because something intangible has changed.

Realistic – For me, the person choosing the goal, and in the time period and measures set for achieving it. I believe I can actually do this. It might be a stretch, but it is possible.

Timely – I have named a time by which I will have achieved the objective.

It is particularly helpful to have a set of SMART objectives to work toward. These are my objectives and are best derived after a thorough investigation of personal values, vision and a look at the future using the five- and/or two-year pictures. It would be a good idea to read the affirmation tool (page 115) before I start this work.

"What would have to have changed for me, both personally and professionally, if I were to look back three years from now, in order for me to be totally satisfied with my progress?" (Dan Sullivan, strategic coach)

A soulful, heartfelt answer to that question will put me in the zone, for sure. I use the work done so far. I collect a number of possible outcomes from all the work done up to now. I needn't be concerned about the SMART part of it yet. The quantity doesn't matter, but the true connection with what I really want does matter, a lot. I write what comes newly to mind and from the work so far. I ask, "What is really important here?" I write the answer to the question *as a result,* tangible or otherwise, and we'll get to the to-do list soon enough. For example, "I earn $150,000 in the year 200x working under 20 hours per week." That is already even pretty close to SMART format, too. Now define work, etc.

Once I have a list, I just let it sit. I revisit it on occasion and add to it or refine it, but don't erase or toss anything. It all has some message in it, just for me. I can then start to group items around themes and around common activities. If I notice connections between items I combine them or draw an arrow between them.

This is not meant to be a quick task. I let it take time. A few days? OK. A week? OK. A few weeks? OK. Not every element of the original visualization needs to have a SMART string connected to it. In the end, the number of fully developed SMART objectives often makes for an alarmingly short list. No gold star for a long list. I give myself permission to go for the heartfelt, critical few dominoes that make the biggest difference.

There will come a time when I just feel done. I follow the format and develop my own set of SMART objectives for the next few years.

Congratulations! This is further than 90 percent of the population ever gets in goal-setting. Ever. So a hearty congratulations!

Personal Acknowledgment Break

Time for another pause. I engage the following slowly and notice my entire response. These statements are a guided experience. I am gentle with the statements, letting them have their effect.

Where am I? I have explored myself and possibly discovered a part of my Self. I "see" better what is important, what is truly me, and see it more clearly than I have ever seen it before. I have destinations that are whole and of my own choosing because they feel right, and not because I am "supposed to" want them. I know more about why I want these goals than I have ever known anything about myself. I will recognize the achievement of these goals because I have experienced the results in advance. I am in a powerful place, that of co-creator of my own future. I now design my life, no more a victim of circumstance, but a being in connection with my Self. I am where I am meant to be, where *I belong,* living my life on purpose, using my whole being to decide my next action.

Statement of Being – Personal Vision and Mission

My way of being is the way I am when I am my whole and magnificent Self. My way of being is what enables me to have a vision of my purpose and to accept the mission of acting upon it. My *statement of being* is my source.

We are at the door of our destination, as guided by the personal work done up to now. We are now but this one step away.

What image do I get when I hear, "Now there's a person with a mission"? Do I envision a person so focused and clear on what she wants and where she's going that I'd better not get in her way? Determination, drive, focus and passion – against all odds, this person is getting things done. It is infectious and I even want to help this person. How do I get some of that for me?

We all exist for a reason. I am meant to contribute in my own away and what I have to offer is valuable, even essential, to the overall unfolding of the universe as it should. Lofty? Maybe. But what if it is even partly true?

I am here on earth to "be" something important, something vital.

We move from objective, to goal, to next, to … the ne xt promotion, more peace, a bigger house, whatever accomplishment is next. But what's it all about? And what is it about this model that says I have to do 4,378 things before I can get to … where? What if I could be "there" right now and always? What is attractive about that?

Where is "there"? It is my place of calling. It is my purpose in life, the reason I exist. "There" is a way of being that makes me whole and gives me meaning.

I don't answer these questions yet. I just read them:

What is my purpose in life? What am I offering the world?

What about my offering makes the world a better place?

What uniquely qualifies me to do this vitally important thing?

> What is the essence of my way of being?
>
> What will be happening (for me and the rest of the world) when I am fulfilling my call, when I am being my Self?

How may people are able to answer these questions off the top of their heads? Many won't even understand the questions. If responses don't emerge now, don't be concerned. These same questions appear again, after further personal research work. But what if I can answer and do so with conviction? Am I not now a "person with a mission"?

And because I know it clearly I am "in it," "there," "on track," fulfilling my personal calling. I need to be my Self in order to fulfill my mission with confidence and thus to be (not become, but be) all that my vision tells me I am.

When I am my Self, the doing needed to fulfill my mission is easy. It's good. It is very, very good.

There is no surefire way to uncover one's personal way of being, but there are some approaches that help to uncover it. They are described below. They are all variations of asking what is truly important, compelling, vital *to me?* We can use the approaches to get ever closer. The closer to "on purpose" I get, the closer to being my Self, the more I feel like all work is play and time concerns me no longer.

The Wheel of Life

This section includes a picture of a pie or wheel that has eight spaces in it. Each is labeled with an area of life that may be important to most people. A ten (outside rim) is perfect, nirvana, and a one (the center) is so low that it could not possibly be worse. I score the wheel for myself. No need to be overly precise or "right," I'm just getting a sense of where I feel I am at this moment.

Each category is described below the drawing (from *Co-Active Coaching* by Whitworth/Kinsey-House/Sandahl).

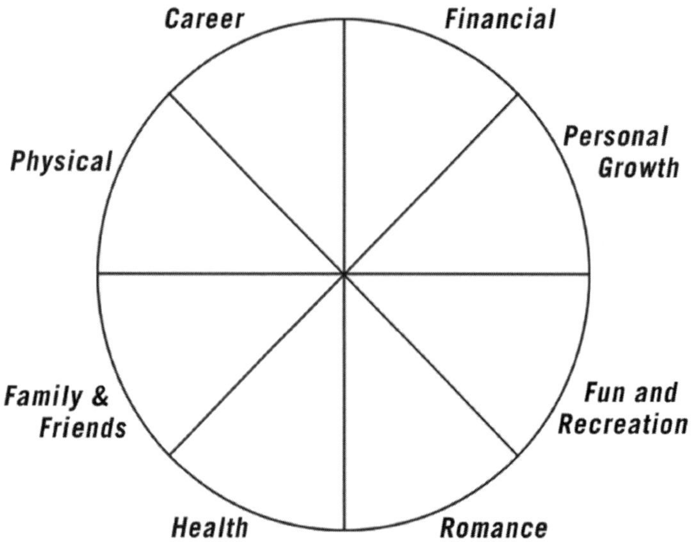

Financial – How am I doing in the money department? How close am I to being "on" here? A measure of how much time I worry over money.

Personal growth – Includes ongoing intellectual growth, spiritual satisfaction and all learning areas. How satisfied am I here?

Fun and recreation – Laughing-out-loud moments and being happy in doing something that I just happen to like, *for me*. What is my fun quotient?

Family and friends – Compared to my ideal mix, where am I in my relationships – quantity, quality, variety, etc.

Romance – The main squeeze in my life, how is that going? What does better look like in this area? Where am I between nirvana and hopeless?
Career – That activity I do for most of my day, which most of us would refer to as our work and that we often associate with our accomplishment in the world.
Health – The level of satisfaction with my sense of well-being; fitness, ability, outlook, demeanor.
Physical environment – Where I spend most of my time, the workplace and my home, from a material kind of comfort/satisfaction perspective, including the commute between the two places (very subjective and personal). This is a place to include the cranky folks in some of my environment, e.g., the job could be great (career) but the interpersonal atmosphere in the workplace may be toxic.

Now I notice what areas seem to be really working for me. I spend a little time to notice for all eight slices of the pie and redraw the outer rim in each sector at the level that I have scored it between 1 at the center and 10 at the original outer rim.

Next, I note what is not working or needs adjustment. Again, I sit with all eight items, giving them all of my attention for a bit of time.

In other words, I provide some justification for the score that I put down for each category. I learn to understand what I value, where I believe things are with me, right now, and the underlying parts that have brought me to those scores. This is interesting. After all, it is all about me, the real me.

The scores are not chiseled in stone. They could move around, even from day to day. However, they do indicate the areas that are important to me, at least right now. Important how? The lowest scores tell me what I want more of, and those are important. The highest scores tell me what I am more OK with and where I am probably now putting my efforts. So they are important too. If I do the analysis and notice what I have written about each, there will likely be some information about what is really calling to me and lots of things about where to look further to uncover my place, where I am whole. The real question becomes, "What will it take to get me to a wheel with all tens?"

Is that even possible? Maybe not, but wouldn't it be great to get close, even for a while? I notice that what gets me to a ten is probably not the same as what gets others to a ten. This is personal. I give myself permission to take care of only me in this.

I take my time and score the wheel a few times over a period of a month or so. I try it cold each time, not just editing the last version. This is fun and easy and is teaching me about me.

Probing Questions

In my quest to uncover a personal statement of being, it is most helpful to know what "doing" my mission is going to accomplish. What does it look like when I am "there"? The foregoing gets me closer, for sure. In addition to these questions I have already worked on answering, what can I say about the following?

> Who in the world seems to be most of what I want to be? My response could be many people and I might just want certain pieces of each. What are those pieces?
>
> What, exactly, do they seem to have that is so attractive to me? What are they doing that I want to do more of, or to do better?
>
> What am I missing or what do I need, in order to be more like them? If I decided today to do what they do, at least as well as they do it, what needs to happen?

My Magnificence

My answers to the questions above give many ideas of how I would recognize magnificence in myself. Yes, magnificence. We are not used to hearing such words to describe ourselves. Well, just for the fun of it, I approach this with a "what if" attitude. What if I were magnificent? Or what *could* I be doing if I already am magnificent? And if I am still not comfortable, I'll just put my imagination in overdrive and laugh out loud.

I list the ten, or so, people who are most important to my life. I then describe beside each a perfect interaction between them and me, listing only my side of the interaction. That is, independent of what they say/do, what is my preferred and perfect way of dealing with each of them? What am I thinking, saying, doing and feeling while interacting with these important people?

What is it like when I am my ideal Self? How do I interact with my environment? What am I doing with my mind, my body, my soul? What is happening all around me? I am allowed to check it all out from every direction. The eight categories around the wheel of life diagram are pointers that can help me begin exploring. I play with this awhile and let time percolate the results.

I watch for the gremlin traps that holler, "Who are you to be great?" You know, being great can mean many things:

> I am a listener, a wonderful intimate; nonjudgmental, open, always available to any and all, without conditions and always with joy to just provide. *I am "the listener" who contributes to the greatness of everyone I meet.*

Whew. I want to meet "the listener."

> *I am the mirror that shows each person more of their magnificence.*

Yes, I want some of that.

> *I am the breath that expands the consciousness of the universe.*

Yes! So refreshing to be around this person. Gimme some of that.

> *I bring the steady hand to the tiller in my interactions with my fellow beings.*

No stress around this person.

And the list goes on. Where am I in this list of essential beings? What am I when I am whole and my Self? What do I crave so much in my experience of the world? What something do I want more than anything and so treasure when I recognize it in others? If I could give one, just one, gift to the world, what the world needs most, what would that be?

Now I am ready to answer the five questions from page 80 (repeated again below).

> What is my purpose in life? What am I offering the world?

> What about my offering makes the world a better place?

> What uniquely qualifies me to do this vitally important thing?

> What is the essence of my way of being?

> What will be happening (for me and the rest of the world) when I am fulfilling my call, when I am being my Self?

The Statement

What am I now committed to be? Yes, I may mess up along the way, but what am I like when I am not messing up, when I am in flow and, yes, magnificent? In my magnificence I am definitely allowed to mess up because that too is a beautiful part of me. Without that lovely messy part I would not be human.

I begin a statement (or statements) for each of the eight categories on the wheel of life (page 82). I am fairly quick. Dwelling to uncover a perfect answer won't help here. I let it just roll out as it comes to mind. I return to each set of statements and ask, "If I did this, what would I be?" This may feel funny for some of them, but I keep going, relishing the ones that work and skimming over the others.

What I now have is a great beginning to a personal statement of being. I write a paragraph that starts with, "I am …"

I can sprinkle in some clarification as needed to explain what I am doing among all of the "being" and let it sit for a week or two. When I revisit it, I just feel the message and know my Self. There is no gold standard to compare to. The "right" statement is the one that feels familiar and possible *to me.*

> Example (carried in a briefcase and read often for over ten years):
>
> I am honest, cheerful, generous, stable and competent.
>
> My mind is clear and relaxed so that I can first understand what I encounter and then decide my responses, rather than act from habit, assumption or impulse. My body is healthy, flexible and active.

> I eat, drink, exercise and sleep to the maintenance and betterment of the temple of my soul.
>
> I am one who is pure of heart and at peace.
>
> I enjoy life and accept others as integral to my fulfillment and happiness; therefore, I show each person acceptance and thoughtfulness.
>
> I "listen" for HIS direction and choose to follow it.
>
> My "self" in business is the same as elsewhere and, because of the attributes described, every business that I touch is successful at a deep core level, allowing regular and generous giving to employees and the community to be a part of the business routine.

From Being to Mission

When I am my whole Self, when I am being what I have been called to be, one question that arises is, "What am I to do with all of this being?" Having discovered more of what I have been called *to be,* what am I called *to do?*

> What if my personal mission is to be my Self
> in whatever I choose to do?

I'd like to explore that, to give it some space. I want to notice where the exploration is going and notice my own reactions. "Being with" the question, I let it permeate me. I breathe.

If I am a builder, do I build birdhouses or team spirit or computer programs? A lot of time could be spent casting about for the doing that fulfills me. But by being what I have been called to be and by doing what attracts me, choice by choice I will iterate toward the place of doing intended for me, my personal mission toward my personal vision, which is to be my Self.

Rather than going through lists of jobs or careers, I simply go toward fulfillment with every decision, every choice. So never mind those plane tickets to Tibet; I'd rather "be" right where I am. I step into my Self. Now is a perfect time to do that, I mean *to be* that.

In any situation, I ask,
"If everything I do
Is a reflection of what I am,
What must I therefore do with this?"
For every situation in every day,
I notice the results achieved.
I notice my own reactions.
This is "being there."
This is me.
Me at my Natural Edge.

This growth process never ends. We never arrive at a finale. There is always more, always. This is not because we are incompetent, but because we are an extension of the infinite. Thus there is always more, by definition. I may come to a plateau, even experience a dip along the way, but if I continue to choose toward my fulfillment, I continue to get bigger, to be more – and peace, greater and greater, embraces me.

I enjoy my personal work!

What does my Natural Edge look like?

How would I recognize someone who had found, and is living at, their Natural Edge? When I have my Natural Edge, I am aware of and have embraced my personal core values, I have surfaced and stepped into my personal way of being and I have a clear sense of purpose that propels me toward my unique vision. I absolutely know that I belong here on this planet and am welcomed and am needed to do my part in the great plan.

When I inhabit the place that is my Natural Edge, this is what I am like.

To be clear, though, the Natural Edge is my ideal. It is what I am in those moments when I am "in the zone." It is not the way I am 100 percent of the time. I wish. Yet, it is a powerful thing to express what it is like, for me, when I am "in flow." Having written it down has a material effect on the amount of time that I actually am there. I am there more often and for longer as a result of describing my Natural Edge in writing. It is compelling.

The following example is one person's result from the work I have engaged in so far. It is idyllic, but it is what had come from the work, and it sure is attractive to the person who wrote it.

> *This is what my Natural Edge looks like to me.*
>
> *I don't complain* because everything that happens has a purpose and a value for someone. Thus, to complain is to diminish what is of value to another. To complain can also be merely an excuse on my part to ignore what I must learn. To complain for the sake of complaining adds nothing. I define complaining as noticing something that may need to change and then noticing it again and again without either doing anything positive to resolve the matter or resolving to simply let it be.
>
> *I am courageous* in that I know that I cannot fail. When I am clear about my destination and diligently moving toward it, I do what I need to do in order to forge the river or cross the gorge. I know that to do anything less would be unfulfilling and would gnaw at me, stealing from my happiness. I am fulfilled in the pursuit of what I know to be right – in my view – and truly valuable. I am comfortable with short and long steps toward my goals and also with the occasional standing still or even falling back. I happily keep going.

I am consistently my Self. I am happy with me as I am, so don't need to bend myself to please you. I get my confidence from within. I don't expend energy being something on the outside that I am not on the inside.

I am positive because I know that where I am going and where I am are the right places for me. When I know that I am on my true path, you can say what you will and I will still smile and persevere and maintain high spirits. The knowing comes from understanding what I am here to do (to contribute) and from knowing what about that mission is vital to the world. When I know that, really know it, I am invulnerable.

Life is easy. All work is play. Each task is a source of pleasure because I know that it is another positive step toward delivering my gift. I am experiencing a wonderful adventure. I am moving toward an unimaginably great treasure. I am preparing the soil for the arrival of the harvest. It is exciting and no task is unworthy of me.

I speak well of others and of myself because there is only Acceptance, thus each person is just fine in the way they are. There is no performance anxiety because everyone does the very best they can, always. When I recognize that this is so, I can only speak well of others and this begins by speaking well of myself. This "being gentle with me" allows me to laugh at me (and thus others) and to enjoy rather than doubt the events around me.

I listen to understand and am curious about your life journey and how that works for you and how it connects with mine. Listening genuinely comes naturally. You have my full attention, without preconception and without my struggle to prepare a stunning response. I want to know who you are.

I say yes when I mean yes and no when I mean no. There is no need to hide, or to artificially please someone, by saying a certain thing or being a certain way. I have absolute certainty about what I am doing and feel no need to justify or apologize. I listen to refine my beliefs and to learn more about the world and simply respond with my truth.

I know where I am going. My way of being, my purpose, my vision, my mission is all that I need in order to stay on course. I can stay on course because I have clarity about my destination and about the importance of moving toward it.

I make decisions easily, very easily, because I have a simple way to test each decision. Is this going to get me closer to my goal? Is this on or off my chosen path? Is doing this consistent with my ideal Self? Even, is this choice of language, these words I am about to speak, consistent with the real me?

Do I now know this person? Can I imagine how they would act in almost any situation? Would I like to meet this person?

Life is a huge buffet. I can have as much as I wish of anything that the buffet has to offer. As with taking from the food buffet, taking from the life buffet has consequences. Too much of anything usually ends up in illness. Not enough of some things can make the whole affair rather uninteresting. Learning what are the best things for me is the adventure of living. Finding and keeping my Natural Edge – that place where I am whole and fulfilled – is the goal. I pursue it by being it, most of the time. Well, OK, some of the time. But it is more of the time now than it used to be and that is really great, for me.

Critical in the above is the statement about pursuing. The buffet is always ready. If I do not get off of my chair, pick up a plate and walk over, choose and put items onto my plate, I will starve. I, and I alone, will fill my plate with good choices, in perfect proportions, to fulfill me. I must act.

Describing My Own Natural Edge

I have read the example, but what does my *own* Natural Edge look like?

I outline my Natural Edge in writing that is revealing and empowering for me. The form of description matters little. The content is expected to be idyllic. After all, it describes me while I am in my magnificence. Opportunities to notice what my own magnificent Self is like include:

> Situations in which I notice that I don't agree with what another is doing/saying/not doing. A situation that I would, if only I could, and sometimes actually do, handle differently and in the different handling would move the world toward its intended state again rather than adding to its wrongness (in my opinion, based on what I believe). What am I when I easily and naturally do that different thing?
>
> Any time I look back upon my own actions with disquiet. "Something about that did not really add up to helpful," I say to myself. What would add up to helpful? Doing that helpful thing is being my magnificent Self. What am I when I easily and naturally do that "adding up to helpful" thing?
>
> People I have admired, even if for only a moment. What I admired was goodness, as defined by me. It was what I actually am when I am "in the zone," mirrored for me in others. It is worthy of my

striving for. What am I when I no longer need to admire from afar but actually "am" admirable?

Where people struggle, and succeed, in doing the one thing, sometimes the hard thing, that will be best in a given situation, acting above and beyond the call of duty. Those actions that catch me saying, "Gee I don't know if I could have done that, but I do know, somehow, that I would want to have done it." What am I when I just do those actions easily and naturally?

Situations in which I may not be fully honoring myself and thus feel uncomfortable. Ask, "What action/understanding would allow me to feel totally welcome and comfortable here?" What would I have *to be* in order to regain comfort? What would I have *to do* in order to regain comfort? What is the magnificent part of me that is suppressed here?

I add in a list of attributes I would like to have if I were a superhero here to demonstrate right living. Not moralizing or judging about right living, but living in the way that is best at teaching me the truth about me and us – the real me, the real us in that place of absolute Acceptance. What am I *being?*

The world is a better place with me in it.

If that is true, what do I do that adds positively, and even teaches, in every interaction with my fellow human beings?

What do I just know is true about how to act? What do I completely believe that sustains my feeling of fulfillment?

I reread the results of this last personal work sequence and see what I am like when I live at my own Natural Edge. Cool.

In facing off with these provoking personal questions, I come to know myself better and come to understand that I have a meaningful place here on earth. This is a wonderful gift I give to myself. Having given it, I am more. Thus, when we meet, I have more to give to you; a gift I give to you.

KEEPING

KEEPING

My Natural Edge

The work I have done so far has exposed some of my Natural Edge. I can see it now. I have seen/experienced some moments of fulfillment. What would it be like to be at my Natural Edge all of the time? As I unfold my understanding of this way of being, what can I do to hold it and to expand it?

I cannot give what I do not have. Thus, it is better for the world if I am the best that I can be. I can only love you to the extent that I can conceive of love for myself.

Self-actualization and self-fulfillment are acts of love, love of the world, starting with myself.

Having worked through Finding and then Deciding, I now see more of my Natural Edge.

Keeping, and growing, my Natural Edge is partly a matter of habit-building and partly a matter of being. Did I read that right? I need to build a habit, after having worked to get past habit, off automatic and into the present moment?

Noticing, the opposite of living on automatic, is the kind of habit to foster. When I am noticing I am more likely to be at my Natural Edge, in a place where "being" my whole Self is a conscious choice. To act always in the way of being that keeps me in my calling is the objective. Ahhh, my intent. Intention begets attention and attention begets action.

So how do we do that?

The norm for us humans is that we are attracted to things that are new. Excitement rises and positive anticipation motivates. The advertising industry knows this, so it is pretty normal to include the word "new" in an advertisement. Once something is old, or even just familiar, we start to lose interest. A new skill, like using a clutch in driving a standard-shift car, becomes a subconscious skill and is no longer an experience but simply something that is done.

My "intent" ultimately defines my result.

The intent referred to here is the underlying true intent. Someone asks, "How are you?" I respond with, "I am fine." What was my intent? I may have intended to get rid of this person by giving the very least cause to stop and converse. I may have intended otherwise, and if so, the tone, the level of eye contact and a whole host of other factors that accompany the words would be different with this other intent. My long-term intent with respect to keeping my Natural Edge is the largest factor in determining what I will achieve in that area.

What is my intent?

What does that mean for my commitments regarding the experiences I have had and those yet to be had on my journey through this book?

With this intent clear in my mind, what is now possible for me?

The following list and subsequent explanatory sections provide a few practices that help keep me present and fresh:

1. Meditation – to maintain present-moment connection and peacefulness.
2. Visualization – to generate and regenerate the advance memory of my ideal future.
3. Affirmation – to accelerate the transition of visualization into reality.
4. Personal fulfillment plan – write to maintain focus.
5. Inquiry – to get past blockers and maintain presence.

Meditation

Many methods, same objective. Meditation is a method to quiet my mind of the constant prattle, the endless parade of thoughts, some useful, many just fillers. The basic concept is to occupy my mind with a single, simple task, like watching the breath. So doing quiets the mind and eventually I can "not think," rather I can listen. What am I listening for? Well, for the Spirit, the universal subconscious, the answer.

There are many excellent books and tapes that teach basic meditation. Personally speaking, I particularly enjoyed Jon Kabat-Zinn's *Wherever You Go, There You Are.* Here are three forms of meditation that I find especially beneficial.

Bungee Cord Exercise Meditation

One of the most interesting forms of meditation that I have come across is used in exercise, such as jogging. I imagine that a bungee cord is connected to my chest and as I inhale, I imagine the cord pulls me a little. As I exhale, I imagine the person holding the other end takes up the slack so they can again pull me on the inhale. The effect is to keep me "on the breath," as they say in meditation talk. My mind is focused in the present moment, not fuming over something past or predicted in the future. I am "here." In addition, my running will improve in that I will run more smoothly and achieve a better time. This is a great help when running a long distance, for instance. The method can be adapted to cycling, swimming or almost any activity involving repetitive motion. Very simple. Very refreshing.

Manifesting Meditation

Not all meditation is silent. Wayne Dyer suggests a form that has me make a sound with each out breath (there's that breath again). Make the sound of God/Creator/Source for twenty minutes in the morning while concentrating the mind on the so-called third eye, at the center of the forehead between the eyebrows, and concentrate on experiencing the feeling I will have when I have manifested the result, that which I believe I want. I suspend my disbelief in my ability to manifest anything I want. I picture what I believe I want and then *anticipate the feelings that result from having it*. That feeling is what I hold in my third eye as I make the sound. Finally, I detach from the outcome and let the universe provide in its own way.

The morning sound, the sound of Creation, is ahhhhhhhhh. In the evening I make the sound of gratitude with each out breath for twenty minutes. The sound of gratitude is ohmmmm. I concentrate on my feelings of gratitude for all that has already been manifest in the world and close the meditation session by combining the Creation sound with the gratitude sound to, with the breath, speak shaaaaaa loooohhm, which is an ancient word for peace. This meditation is physically stimulating as well as mentally relaxing. I quite like it. A good one to do with children too, because they are not as inhibited as we adults seem to be. The sound is itself soothing and the result is, again, refreshing.

For a more thorough description and the background on this technique refer to the Nightingale Conant tape set *The Secrets to Manifesting Your Destiny*, by Dr. Wayne W. Dyer.

Loving Kindness Meditation

The Loving Kindness Meditation is especially good because one can do it almost anywhere and anytime, aloud or silently.

I first came across this form around the time of the fall of the Berlin wall. I read that this meditation was the reason that the wall fell. Since that time I have noticed it in various writings and have found a tape set – titled *Loving Kindness Meditation* by Sharon Salzberg, available from www.soundstrue.com – that describes the meditation sequence and some of its origins in Buddhist ritual.

The idea is straightforward: Ask for what you want.

The recommended sequence is as follows:

May I have safety?
May I have mental health?
May I have physical health?
May I have ease of well-being?

It is suggested that I ask for these in sequence and repeatedly for twenty minutes twice a day for one month. Then I expand the "ask" to include someone close to me, someone who I love, for instance:

May Mary have safety?
May Mary have mental health?
May Mary have physical health?
May Mary have ease of well-being?

So now I ask for myself and then for Mary, again repeated pairs, for twenty minutes, twice per day.

After a few weeks I expand the sequence to include someone I know only as an acquaintance. Again, now with the three – myself and Mary and the other – I repeat for two twenty-minute periods.

Third, I expand the sequence to include someone I don't know, maybe the bus driver or the lady at the post office.

Fourth, I add someone that I feel is separated from me; this person has not been a friend and may even be considered an enemy. This is an important part of the meditation so I choose someone I feel most separated from for best effect.

Finally, I include the people of the world in the string.

I can alter the names of the people in the string at any time, except that I always start with myself. I can do this meditation while washing the dishes or driving my car or walking the dog. Any time is fine, and I don't need to sit in a specific position or be alone in a special place. The key is to do it regularly and consistently. I like to do it when I am riding my motorcycle; I am alone, doing the meditation does not impair my safety and it just so happens that the drive to town is about twenty minutes.

In my own practice of this form of meditation, I have noticed that the original form could be stronger as an affirmation. So I have changed it to suit my own view of what would work best for me. I guess I am an overzealous type sometimes – part of my beautiful Self ❀.

First, I have changed the form into first-person present tense. Second, I have expanded the statements to be more specific. Here are my variations on the basic idea:

I know that I am safe.
I enjoy excellent mental health, continuing to learn and grow in wisdom every day. I act from my growing wisdom.
My physical health is excellent. I move with vitality and enjoy full use of my entire body.
I live with daily increasing equanimity and thus enjoy ease of well-being.

In the first one I have used the word "know" because "I have safety," although a great affirmation, could still leave me in doubt. I could have it and not realize it. The certainty of knowing is incredibly powerful. In the mental and physical health areas I have described the way I am because of having those gifts. I could be physically healthy and even vibrant and be in a wheelchair, so I made it clear that I am up and moving fully. In the last part I have given myself an instruction to "live with daily increasing equanimity" as the path to get the carrot of "ease of well-being." By making the equanimity "daily increasing" I am active in increasing my ease of well-being.

I developed this sequence over a period of about five weeks while on an extended motorcycle trip. It didn't just pop up fully formed. It will probably move again as I grow my way through life. It needn't be static.

What next? I have the meditation and I say it every day. So what? Well, the important adjunct here is to ask myself, "If I know that I am safe, what is my reaction to this?" "This" is whatever is in front of me or on my mind, right now. Posing the "if" question puts rocket fuel into applying this meditation. The "if" causes me to come to the present moment and to choose my reaction to whatever is in front of me or on my mind, right now, based on what I am being because of the affirmative meditation.

Anyone can enjoy making their own Loving Kindness Meditation. The process includes sharing good wishes with others, even those we might label as enemies. The Loving Kindness Meditation will definitely be life-changing in a most positive way. And it is so easy to incorporate daily. Choose a trigger event to start, something like the drive to the office, or whatever works.

Other Meditations

There are thousands of meditation methods, some with a mantra, some with a special position to hold during meditation, many variations on the basic theme of opening to the Spirit and becoming more centered/relaxed/aware of my Self. Meditating creates, sustains and enlarges the foundation for enduring positive change. Personally, if I had to choose and foster only one habit, this would be it.

Re-Visualization

In order to generate the dream of my ideal future with minimum interference from the gremlin and other detractors to my magnificence, it is helpful to first address my ideal as if it were a dream. Most detractors will have little to say about a dream compared to what they might say about a "plan" or, heaven forbid, a statement of commitment. Besides, dreams can be fun. Dreams are easy and have no rules. Anything goes, even if it is illogical.

Do I have an issue to address? I go to the future and dream about what it will be like when it is all solved – not just solved but solved perfectly. The habit of reaching first for the ideal outcome is called "the solution-seeking reflex." Now that is a great habit to have. I reach first for ideal solutions from a space of infinite possibility and zero restrictions, far better than picturing all of the roadblocks and naysayers along the way.

I get inside the dream and walk around. I spread my arms and laugh out loud. I play. For goodness sake, play. I experience possibility. Eventually parts of the dream will start becoming reality. Those visualizations are seeds of reality. The universe has everything in it. All I have to do is go looking and I will find it. So bit by bit my dream comes into reality and I move from dreaming to believing and finally to knowing.

The original visualization sample is in the "Deciding" section (page 66). I use visualizations for little steps as well as the life-changing leaps. Well why not? I am strengthening my solution-seeking reflex.

Writing a Personal Fulfillment Plan

A personal fulfillment plan might be derived from the section titled "Statement of Being – Personal Vision and Mission" (page 79):

1. What is my purpose in life/what am I offering the world?
2. What about my offering makes the world a better place?
3. What uniquely qualifies me to do this vitally important thing?
4. What will be happening (for me and the rest of the world) when I am fulfilling my call?

There is immense power in writing answers to such questions. I write my answers and just leave them in a drawer. A few months later, or whenever the Spirit moves me, I write the answers again, afresh, without rereading the earlier answers. If I edit a prior version, the range of what is possible is corralled by that prior plan. For maximum range, I write afresh with no regard for the earlier versions. I let the growth I have experienced in the interim bear fruit and let it enhance my personal fulfillment plan.

Writing and rewriting the plan, and doing so afresh every time, has the effect of advancing the plan – and the writer – toward "there." So write and write often.

Inquiry

The inquiry is an open question that I am unlikely to have a quick answer to. It is crafted to help me explore a topic in an experiential way. The question is engaging and somehow far reaching for me. The time to turn to an inquiry is when I am not sure about something but am curious or feel engaged by it. Maybe I am infuriated over something. I use an inquiry about "permission" in this situation to unlock the fury.

For example, I'm feeling stuck in the muck, not moving, wanting an action step. There is disquiet. Something about getting out of the surrounding gremlins and other toxic blockers around me on the field of life. So I start to banter about possible inquiry candidates.

> Where is the opening?
> Where is the goal line?
> What is between the opening and me?
> *What does the opening look like?
> How do I open it?
> How do I notice the opening?

And variants on the *:

> What does the opening have to offer?
> What does the opening feel like? Bull's-eye!

I choose the question with the * for further exploration because of the energy that I notice when it arises. The bull's-eye was evident in my reaction – no magic in the words per se, but in the connection, for me, to those words.

The "how" questions tend to bring me to my head rather than deepening my understanding of life as it relates to me. The "where" questions tend to be like the "how" questions. "What" questions seem to be most suitable because they beg for input in a wider way than "how" and "where." It is good to explore awhile for a visceral reaction to the questions. "What is the first step?" can then evolve into the much more intriguing and moving question, "What is the second step," which blows past all the "ya buts" associated with the first step. A great inquiry.

The inquiry is a plaything, a question that I engage with an attitude of "what if" and innocuous brainstorming. Nothing too serious. I let the question arise and then merely notice the answers. Nothing to do. Nothing to write down or to count or to report back. I just play and notice. I launch the inquiry question often and notice. Things will "pop" as I play, valuable things, insightful and useful. Things about me that maybe I didn't fully realize.

A few variants on the original inquiry, just for fun, might include:

What is opening? (Note the many meanings possible here.)
What is scary about opening? (acknowledging and naming fears)
What is already open? (positive noticing)

For a further example of an inquiry string on the topic of "in the flow," please visit the web site www.yournaturaledge.com/personalfulfillment .

Here is a different inquiry with a set of variants:

What about action is so attractive to me?
What does action give me?
What about action hurts me sometimes?
What is the juicy, exciting part of being in action?
What does staying in action protect me from?
What is my definition of real action?
What are ten other words for action?

Another set:

What is the resistance to caring for me?
What does resistance feel like?
What is the very best thing about resistance?
When does resistance hurt me?
Where do I use resistance in my life?
What about resistance is so seductive?

What is the cost of resistance?
Who expects resistance from me?

Some of these variants don't follow the "what" question form. It is not a rule that "what" is best, it is just an observation that most effective inquiries seem to start with "what."

An inquiry/bumper sticker/fridge magnet is a playful and extraordinarily effective way to get unstuck from a view that seems to have only one choice (an unhappy choice) or to open an area that feels unknown. Mostly, it is an exploration tool that stimulates my intent with more and richer possibilities.

Above all, an inquiry is a plaything. So play.

Persistence

Our human capacity for learning and working ebbs and flows. Sometimes we seem to have infinite energy and at other times we just don't want to get out of bed. This is natural and ordinary, so why fight it? Allow time to assimilate and balance rest with a sensible level of persistence (not to be confused with forcing).

> Nothing in the world can take the place of persistence.
> Talent will not; nothing is more common than unsuccessful men with talent.
> Genius will not; unrewarded genius is almost a proverb.
> Education will not; the world is full of educated derelicts.
> Persistence and determination alone are omnipotent.
>
> —Calvin Coolidge

I persist, not in level of drive and force, but in my intent.

Persistent intent is the underlying source of all results.

Intent, combined with persistence and the gentleness that comes with an understanding of the ebb and flow of energy in my human form, facilitates a level of overall consistent achievement that very few manage to maintain. This potent concoction gives me maximum power.

"What is my intent?"

Assimilation

We do not learn by inundation. All things in nature have a rhythm, a rising, a falling, a moment of quiet and stillness where nothing seems to be happening. The trees lose their leaves and go quiet over winter. The animals (all of us) move through time in cycles of flood and ebb and stasis intermixed. Over time we come to understand what we are, and where we are in our journey, fully enough to accept the next flood.

It does little good for a virtuoso to explain everything they know in a matter of days. I will not be able to duplicate even a fraction of the skill they have developed over a lifetime. I need time to assimilate. Sometimes that does not look like action or progress. I go to sleep with a problem rolling around in my head and awake with the answer. I practice an instrument for months and one day I play well and easily what seemed impossible before.

The mind tells the body what to do. We are habitual beings. We learn and make the habits that we need in order to live. The small conscious mind concentrates on a new ability and, given enough time and practice, finally absorbs it into a habit. The subconscious has been programmed.

If I insist on moving forward before I am truly ready, I undermine my future success. I need to completely assimilate the basic dance step and do it naturally, almost without thinking, before I can fully absorb the variations of the dance. My mental capacity is still counting, "one-two-three," rather than giving due attention to the finer points of "the impetus step" of ballroom waltz.

In a period of personal searching and growth, there will be times when little seems to be happening. It is not necessary to fill these times with activity. In fact, it may be best to just let those times be empty and allow the subconscious to absorb the program, so far, and let the present program run again and again. This allows me to establish a plateau, a place for my mind to launch from when the next "rise" (change) is begun. It allows me to try variants and to experience the texture of the new behavior, letting me gain confidence.

If I insist on constant activity, my mind does not fully absorb and the solid foundation needed for enduring positive change is denied an opportunity to set. This weakens the skyscraper as "new" story upon story is added to the structure. The changes along the way, if added to too soon, are still fragile and vulnerable to being lost.

Setting my foundation – assimilation – is assisted by review, by practicing and experimenting with variants of the changes I have already accepted, by self-congratulations about all that I have achieved thus far and by simply waiting until the dissonance, the hunger that inevitably fuels change, begins to stir again. It will. I will soon enough be ready to move to the next change if only because the last one was so satisfying that I want another.

And why not?

Rest and assimilate.

TOOLS

TOOLS

and Helpful Anecdotes

Affirming

An affirmation is a statement about what I believe I am (in my view). It is also an order to my subconscious to make it so. Two possibilities arise. I believe the statement to be already true, so my mind does not have to do anything, or I do not believe the statement is true, so my mind gets to work to make it true. The second situation is powerful for getting me to where I want to be.

Everything I am today is a result of an affirmation I made before today.

Yes, everything.

How I see myself is constantly reinforced by my self-talk, which is a string of affirmations reinforcing the way things are for me. For the most part, people do not believe that everything they are today is a result of a "request" or affirmation. Yet, if I observe others and notice the way they talk about themselves it is usually apparent that they are what they affirm.

We tend to label each other – pro, loser, geek, joker, winner, jock, prude, etc. People act in a certain way that evokes a label and do so consistently. I see myself as a joker, so I act like a joker. You call me a joker and everything is in equilibrium. But I don't often *purposely* affirm all parts of myself. Rather, I roll along through my days, affirming much of my persona on automatic without much *conscious* effort to make the affirmations reflect what I want myself to be.

I could observe myself for a day or two and then decide from the observations alone how I would label me. Try it. What is the scary part of this challenge?

To say, "I weigh 125 pounds," is an affirmation in which the result is "to weigh 125." If I now weigh 132 pounds (or 115) my mind gets to work on adjusting my weight to 125. It does that by noticing different amounts and types of food and opportunities for exercise and so forth. The affirmation is giving me something that I want and that something is fulfilling my view of the world, which I see myself occupying at a weight of 125 pounds. If I don't believe the affirmation, then my mind will cooperate with my skepticism, and the weight will not become the merely stated – and not truly desired – 125 pounds.

If I want to go skydiving and cannot get an image of myself jumping from an aircraft, it will never happen for me. If someone were to say to me that I could do it and I argue that I can't, then that is an affirmation blocker. Cannot skydive. Got it, says my subconscious. It then makes sure that I notice all the articles, news stories and coffee talk about back injury and other perils, on up to death, that result from skydiving. Of course, the physical requirements of this and that acrobatic skill, the cost of the course and the equipment are also highlighted at every turn. No, I cannot skydive. An affirmation needs fertile ground to be effective. Cannot is the opposite of possibility. No affirmation here.

Where do statements like "life is attitude" come from? Why are some people afraid of some things and others not? Where does fear come from? Can I affirm fear away?

How is it that some people (admittedly not many) are comfortable around lions? If we talk to one of these people, we find that they speak about lions the way most of us speak about house pets – affirmatively.

> *Everything I am today is a result of an affirmation that I made before today. Yes, everything. My beliefs are the result of affirmations. In fact, my beliefs* are *my affirmations. What I believe I am or can (or cannot) do* is *my world.*

Implanting

If I have a new marching order that I want to make automatic, I can implant it by consciously giving the appropriate order. This kind of thinking is called affirmation or positive thinking or developing what Robert Fritz calls "creative tension" (*The Path of Least Resistance*).

Actually, I can go beyond improving my suite of habits. I can also attract material things to me. Assume I decide that I want to see a red-and-white truck. There is no red-and-white truck presently in view, but I choose to see one. Having received the order, I straighten up, check the rear view mirror, scan from side to side, between buildings and down the side streets. My antennae are up, mind searching. Sure enough, in no time at all, "There's one!" and probably another and another.

Our senses have finite capacity to absorb the information in our environment. We can't absorb it all, so we pay attention to what we need. In driving from A to B, spotting a red-and-white truck could be the entire conscious directive. The subconscious takes care of operating the clutch and it knows the way. (We have gone to B dozens of times.) We never before asked for trucks of any color so couldn't tell what kind, color or quantity to expect.

With the new directive I become attuned and, presto, the trucks appear. Well, not exactly. It is actually only that I am now looking for them, where I wasn't looking for them before. Thus, it will appear that I have attracted a material thing to me.

Can I do this with money? I believe I can.

There is no limit to what we can affirm. If I decide to own a new Harley Davidson motorcycle before such and such a date, I can affirm it today. In my own life I did exactly that. In 1988 I decided that I would own a brand-new Harley in 1993 and that I would pay cash and have enough left over to get the clothes, etc., *and* that I was not going to save my nickels and dimes to get there. Well, in June 1992 a person, whose gift I could never have predicted, gave me the purchase price plus about eight thousand dollars. Many months early and considerably more than I really needed, I had the means to purchase that Harley. I believed that it would (not just could, but *would*) happen, and it did. That seems to be the pattern of affirmations.

Giving Conscious Instructions to the Subconscious

The affirmation is a type of statement or set of statements that causes the mind to go into action on our behalf and thus to get something for us that we want. Certain attributes can give it more strength. It is important not to send mixed or weak signals because the subconscious takes us rather literally. Clear and strong affirmations are required. The components of sound affirmations are described below.

First Person

Affirmations are about only me. All affirmations start with "I," not "you" or "we" or anything else. The subconscious mind has no ability to control others. So it wisely listens only for what I want it to do with me.

Present Tense

I state what I want as if I already have it, present tense. "I have exceptional posture." "I own, and enjoy driving, my 1957 Studebaker Hawk." "I live on an acreage within a forty-minute drive of downtown Halifax." "I weigh 168 pounds." "I earn about $250,000 a year working about three days per week." "It is easy for me to speak in public." "I write well." "I have many friends and numerous acquaintances."

The present-tense requirement is the one most people resist. How can I state something about the future in the present tense?

We tend to resist telling the mind what we perceive to be a lie as though we're fooling our minds into going there, operating under false pretenses. Yet, I don't seem to have any difficulty saying that I am a dummy when I accidentally lock myself out of my car. That is also not true and it *is* an affirmation. If I am in the habit of referring to myself as a dummy, is it any wonder that I seem to so often lock myself out of my car and my house and do other "dumb" things like that?

The mind does tell the body what to do. It doesn't understand "just kidding." Every affirmation, negative or positive, is a genuine marching order.

I suggest that we can, with practice, do as well with positive affirmations as we do now with the negative, with stating what we want as though that is what we *are.* "All" we are doing is giving the mind something good to get to work on.

If stating a present-tense affirmation is difficult, I can try some baby steps first.

At what date in the future might it just be possible to have a certain thing, say, running a mile? I can say, "The date is xxx and I have run a mile today." This is not as powerful as, "I run a mile four days of every week," but does generate some creative tension. It sets up a range of subaffirmations. The mind thinks,

"If I am running a mile, I will need to get running shoes before then and decide on a route and do some serious walking and probably a few quarter- and half-mile runs and ..." Each of those items gets turned into an affirmation. The "to-do" list gets built and off I go.

Another way to deal with the present-tense aspect of affirmations is to use something like what Jose Silva recommends in *The Silva Method.* He suggests that when someone asks me, "How are you?" I respond with "I am better and better." This affirmation sets a direction without a specific end point. The direction is positive and therefore definitely helpful to me. It is present tense but doesn't raise the same resistance as a future state presented in the present tense.

These are both valid interim steps to outright affirmation. The reason we may feel awkward, initially, in stating affirmations is that we don't feel able to do the thing or get the item, which is being affirmed. We have a scarcity and vulnerability view of the world. People who have lots and seem comparatively invulnerable affirm positively as a matter of routine. The following quote, from *A Course In Miracles* by the Foundation for Inner Peace, is about changing the way we see the world. It perfectly explains the sequence of the affirmative process. We do create our own world.

> At first to be but said and then repeated many times;
> and next to be accepted as but partly true, with many reservations.
> Then, to be considered seriously more and more, and,
> finally, accepted as the truth.
>
> —*A Course in Miracles,* lesson 284

Positive Statements

The statements are much stronger when stated in the positive: not "I no longer have poor posture," but "I have exceptional posture"; not "I don't write poorly," but "I write well"; not "I don't want to be alone," but "I have many friends and numerous acquaintances." The mind is listening for instructions and then testing against reality to ascertain whether or not there is anything that needs to be done. The mind seems to respond to the negative statement with confusion, at best. So if I no longer have poor posture, what do I have? A red sports car? What do you want me to do?

It is as though the number of things that I do *not* want is infinite and the conscious mind is so easily overloaded that to tell it one of the infinite things that I do not want is pretty much received with a shrug. Imagine all the things that I don't want and compare that list to the things I do want. It is easy to see why the mind won't even go there when we state our requests in the negative. "I don't smoke as much anymore." Ever hear that one? Chances are that the person making the statement will remain a smoker for quite a while. The person who says, "I am a nonsmoker," has a better chance of becoming a nonsmoker. Further, the person who affirms, "I am healthy," (and who believes that smoking is not healthy) is likely in a good position to stop smoking. How about, "I take good care of my lungs." Now we're talking.

Self-Referenced

I can only affect myself with affirmations. So a statement that includes another, "I write better than Mary," asks the subconscious to use a measuring stick (Mary's ability to write) that it does not have. It only knows me. All instructions are to relate only to me.

Further, it is a fool's errand to affirm something for someone else. Forget it. I cannot create an affirmation to have a friend quit smoking, for instance. How can I give instructions to someone else's subconscious?

Specifics

The affirming instruction needs to define an achievement. "I want to lose weight" is not really an affirmation. It is met with a shrug from the subconscious, "That's nice, so what do you want me to do? You said you want and you already want – no changes needed." "I could ..." has the same non-result.

In Fritz's *The Path of Least Resistance*, he develops creative tension in his instructions. He tells us to describe the future desired clearly enough so that:

1. I will recognize it when I encounter it.
2. I will accept it if it is offered to me.
   [and this is essential]
3. I acknowledge my present reality as it actually is.

Remember the affirmation instruction about the Studebaker? Have I met Fritz's first suggestion with my description so that I will be glad to accept it when it shows up, number two above? I see that only a 1957 model will do. I own it, so I didn't see it in a car show or at a friend's house. I am driving it, so it is not a dilapidated wreck sitting in the corner of a field. In fact, I *enjoy* driving it so it must be in pretty good shape. Do I care what color it is? No. Does it have to be roadworthy and in good enough condition to put a smile on my face? Absolutely. Some details are missing. When? How much? As the affirmation stands, all I know is that I am still young and healthy enough to drive. The rest is open. I can add some or all of those dimensions. When? Do I want it before I am fifty or fifty-five or ...? Am I willing to sell my home or cash in my retirement fund or do I have a fixed ceiling price or do I want it to be given to me or ...? From where? Do I mind traveling five thousand miles to get it or do I want it to be discovered within five hundred miles of home or do I want it to show up in my driveway or ...? The model I want was produced for six years. Can I let go of the year 1957 and improve my chances of getting the car sooner, because there are then more to choose from?

Let's go back to the red-and-white truck. The subconscious does not create the truck. It just heightens all my sensory antennae to find the next red-and-white truck that comes near enough for me to encounter. If I ask for a red-and-white *dump truck* it will take longer because I am being more selective. If I want to see a red-and-white customized pre-1960 pickup truck, it will take longer still. Yet, if I do choose to see such a pickup truck and keep that instruction fresh, the fact that I have not yet seen it develops the "creative tension" that Fritz refers to. Sooner than I expect, there it will be.

Since I did not specify otherwise, it could come to me in a magazine picture at the dentist's office. When I see it I will recognize it and laugh out loud at how the subconscious is both so literal, not to know I meant a real truck as opposed to a picture of one, and at the same time, so brilliant and innovative in meeting my instructions. But getting a paper truck might mean I hadn't done Fritz's points one and two clearly enough if I had been expecting a real truck.

I cannot "mean" I want a real truck; I have to say it explicitly. I also need to let my subconscious find its own way of getting me what I want. I take considerable care to envision the specifics of what I affirm as thoroughly as possible. Yet it is better to hold the vision loosely where possible. If I don't mind what color the Studebaker is, then I don't restrict the vision by specifying it. I get the car sooner that way because the possibilities are greater in number.

Action-oriented

An affirmation is a call to action. It includes verbs, doing words. Imagine we have this little foreman who works in our mind. He has a little hard hat and big thick glasses and a long,

long clipboard on which he writes down all the tasks for the mind to undertake.

Doing means action. To affirm that "I can …" or "I am able to …" or "I will …" does not get any attention from the "to-do" foreman. There is nothing to put on the list. I am inherently "able" to run a mile, probably always have been. So what? Likewise for "I will" run a mile. Without more details the subconscious acknowledges this crystal-ball prediction but doesn't feel the need to bring it about.

My affirmations are stronger and generate more intense creative tension, when I can experience the future in my mind *now*.

Dissonance between my affirmations and the actual present is what goads my subconscious.

To experience the future I need action, movement, wind in my hair, sound of the ocean, smell of the grass, all that. Many humans are visual. When we understand a statement we often say, "I see." So a strong affirmation, for me, is one in which I can "see" the result. I see better in moving pictures than in still photos. An animated view of my desired result makes it rich and can evoke emotion. If I am an aural person, I use sounds to animate and if a tactile person, I use textural images.

I make my affirmation live and experience it in advance. I do all that I can to allow me to recognize it when it actually happens for me.

Emotion

If, when I affirm my desired future, I include feelings in the picture, it becomes more experientially rich, evoking a more whole Self involvement. When I can be excited about the future result, my energy in moving toward it is higher, my attitude is healthier and my positive anticipation greater. "I feel great after my daily one-mile run." "I feel vigorous and happy while running my daily mile and am more alert and energetic for the rest of the day as a result."

Accurate

Be careful what you ask for, you may get it. I say, *will* get it. Accuracy is an important part of giving instructions to anyone. Incomplete details or the use of ambiguous wording can generate disastrous affirmations. This is where brevity can be the enemy. When developing an affirmation, tell it all. Describe the result in luxurious and endless detail. Walk around in it. See it wholly and be specific *where it is important to you.* If a detail does not matter, affirm only results related to it.

For instance, the color of my 1957 Studebaker Hawk is not important. "It is a joy to drive." That suggests that the paint and body are good enough to pass safety inspection and to keep me smiling. Actually, several other model-years are just as acceptable. Hmmmm? Is it the Hawk part that is most important to me, rather than the year? Ahaaa.

Constantly focus on the result, "the what" not "the how." The earlier example of choosing to see an antique truck and finding a picture of one in a magazine at the dentist's office is one where more accurate detail was needed to explain what was really meant. If I had added, "driving down the road," that would have disallowed the magazine picture even though I wouldn't have stated explicitly that I was seeking a real truck. If I add, "hot-rodding down the road," that's emotion and action.

It is important to establish a balance here. More detail allows for less range in options for providing fulfillment of the affirmation. Less detail can generate an unsatisfying result. Be specific *and* wholly accurate on the result and any parts that are vitally important. Then let the subconscious (the universe) do its job. And as I have been doing with the Studebaker example, let it move around a little and let it evolve.

Realistic To Me

Back to the Studebaker for a moment. That vision is very real for me, personally. I can "feel" and "smell" and "see" it. I can, in my mind, experience what it is like to own and drive an antique car. All of these details help me to allay doubts about the realistic possibility of actually attracting my affirmation to me. If I had none of these I may not believe that having the Studebaker is realistically possible for me. I need to check my affirmation to test whether or not I can imagine it as realistic for me.

I cannot imagine owning a full-size railway train. I just don't see it. No desire. No experiential or emotional response. No wanting. No picture. No instruction to the subconscious. It won't happen.

Being realistic and believable to myself is fundamental to effectively directing the subconscious. For example, many people are concerned about their weight. A person affirming a weight of 110 pounds when they have weighed 250 pounds for years will probably find it difficult to see himself at 110. The mind throws up all kinds of doubts and excuses, and although weight may be shed it doesn't stay off. The clear picture in the mind is of a 250-pound person and the picture of someone (probably someone else) weighing 110 is fuzzy, not quite real. Go for the clearer picture because the other is just not as realistic, says the mind.

Two ways to go here include the following: One is to picture 210 pounds and then 180 pounds and then … That is one way, a way recommended by many.

A better way is to explore, "What will I have when I weigh x?" What does that represent? A colleague of mine, when asked about his weight remarks, "I am the ideal weight to support my vigorous lifestyle." Another says, "I eat, drink, sleep and exercise to the betterment of my body, as the temple of my soul." No mention of weight per se, yet both statements show a picture, at least to those who made them, of a desirable body weight. This approach takes the focus off the scales and moves it to a more holistic view. Try this one, "I eat what is good for me," or, "I am proud of how I look." These loosely held fragments are pieces of a holistic instruction that partly defines who I will become, starting from a realistic acknowledgment of who I am now.

When I look around at the people helping themselves at a food buffet, I see an amazing correlation between body type and plate holdings. I can look at mine and see that yes, this food is the type and quantity that a person "like me" would eat. "I eat what is good for me."

Another way to move ourselves toward the necessary believability is to find someone else who has what we are looking to have. If I can't meet them in person at least I can read about them. The weight example is pretty easy. Many people who have the weight I want and enough of them were the weight I am starting at that I can probably meet quite a number who can attest to the reality of my objective. The same holds true for affirming money. I can find millionaires in every city and there are many rags-to-riches examples. Jim Carrey is a famous one. Apparently he slept in cars and was a street person for quite a while. He wrote himself a check for $10 million and dated it in the relatively near future. He put it in his wallet and went about pursuing his career. Sure enough he was able to cash the check and in advance of the date on it. He believed in himself.

A personal example serves well here, too. I was enjoying my daily run one day and was approaching the traffic lights where I usually cross the highway. I saw the light turn green and noticed a slight surge in me to try to make it. But I assessed the distance and concluded that I could not make the light. My whole body just "gave up." The first time my body responded,

"I can make that light, so give a little more effort." The second time it was, "You will never make it, give it up." Is this not exactly what happens with all of our goals? If we think it is possible, we put even more energy into getting it. If not, we basically fold. And my reaction during my run was involuntary. Wow! Better pay attention to my beliefs about what I think is realistically possible for me, or accept a much smaller accomplishment. Think on it.

Realism in my mind for what I am affirming is fundamental to the success of my affirming process.

What I believe I can do is the amount of freedom that I allow myself.

How many people have we met who tell us in every fourth sentence what a loser they are? It is the statement that is doing the most to sustain that image of themselves.

There are ways to explore and expand the bounds of my personal "reality." Try this. Use a fresh copy of the wheel of life found in the "Statement of Being – Personal Vision and Mission" section (page 81) and answer the following for each category around the wheel.

What does the most that I can imagine having look like to me?

What is there? Specifically, what is included?

If 10 percent more were magically delivered and offered to me, could I accept it?

How would I feel accepting it and then saying, "I deserve this"?

What is the most I have ever experienced in this realm of my life? What is the least?

If I asked someone who knows me pretty well, what would they say was the top limit and the bottom limit? (Now go ask them.)

Who would be most upset, or maybe just confused, if I actually attracted and accepted and owned 25 percent more/less of this?

How much of this boundary (upper and lower limit) is absorbed from others and how much is actually my conscious choice?

What's comfortable about this boundary? What's in it for me?

What am I selling myself short on by accepting the boundary where it seems to be at present?

I take time to digest this sequence and "be with" the exercise. I explore as many categories from the pie as I can stay interested in. More is better but even one is good.

What is the correlation between what I actually have in each category compared to my Statement of Being?

What do I need to notice here?

Holistic

We are not one-dimensional beings. Thus, it is important to attend to our whole selves in affirming our future. Because all of my being is created by my affirming, I am best served by affirming in all dimensions, that is, holistically – career, financial, social, spiritual, physical and intellectual. The parts I purposely affirm are purposely actualized. The parts that I leave alone are actualized by happenstance. When I consciously affirm all dimensions of my existence, I achieve my desired balance and an irreplaceable peace results.

Overall affirmations like "I am happy, healthy and wise" are far above the "things" and paint a picture of a result that generates a whole litany of to-do list items. However, overall affirmations are not one-fits-all generalizations. Consider the different person when we change the above to "I am happy, healthy and friendly." Friendly people act in certain ways. I am friendly. I act in the way that friendly people act. Is this different from the other person who is wise? Could be. I take care what I ask for and I am specific in my asking.

Also, all my personal growth work has created my unique vision of my Self. If I affirm using "wise," it is not necessarily the same "wise" as another's.

Components of a Complete Affirmation include:

- First person
- Present tense
- Positive
- Self-referenced
- Specific
- Action-oriented
- Emotional
- Accurate
- Realistic
- Holistic

Some may conclude that any affirmation worth its salt will have all of these explicitly stated. Not so:

I am wise.
I am healthy.
I am happy.
I am love.

These are examples of powerful, high-level, results-focused affirmations. We can test each one against all components of a complete affirmation and, to varying degrees, most are satisfied, at least by implication. But let's not forget that if there is room for interpretation that the to-do list foreman will probably use it. Think of a person in a prison. They may be wise, healthy, happy and a real expression of love. When I read the example just above, did I think of myself in a prison? The parts that matter strongly to me need to be specifically and accurately stated in my affirmation. The crucial element is to wholly see the result that I want and to describe it in the affirming way.

The parent is waiting up for the teenager. It is forty minutes after curfew. The teenager has the car. The way the parent deals with the youth when they arrive will depend more on how they see their relationship when the teen is twenty-five than on any other factor. What is the result the parent wants? If the parent sees a good adult relationship, trusting and confiding in each other at that future time, she may differ from a parent not focusing on that future relationship with regard to how to treat the errant teen. The parent who wants a positive future relationship may affirm, "My side of every interaction with my teen today builds a healthy, trusting future between us."

Now that I know the steps to sound affirmations, I can affirm what I want or leave it to chance. My choice.

Now What?

So I work through all of the foregoing and develop the gold-plated mother of all affirmations, tailored perfectly for me. Now what? The to-do list foreman is habitual. Left to his preferences, "the way I've always done it" creeps in and runs the show. Thus, I need to reprogram my subconscious to make the new way into the automatic way. After all, the way I am now has been a work in progress for how many years? Once I have that new way as automatic then I "am" the new way. A detailed, and thus lengthy, affirmation can be read daily upon waking and before bed and, for that matter, as many other times as I like. Remember the quote from *A Course In Miracles* (lesson 284):

> At first to be but said, ...
> and next to be accepted as but partly true, ...
> and, finally, accepted as the truth.

Simply restating an affirmation brings the picture into the conscious mind and replaces a fresh copy into the subconscious. If the affirmation is whole, eventually, I create the desired new world.

I like to write and rewrite affirmations. Once I have done the work to explore and identify the realistic, experientially rich affirmation of my new Self, it is very powerful to just take a few minutes each day to rewrite it, but not just a memorized copy. I rewrite it by experiencing the result and writing about what I see, feel and do in the new me, today. The day-to-day subject matter is pretty close to the same. Much of the wording may be the same from day to day. Yet, over time the affirmation matures and mellows to become ever more comfortable, like breaking in a new pair of shoes. Some days I may not comment on one or another part of it; rather, I write a luxurious version of only some part(s). Some days I may write only a few key words to describe it all, possibly just the verbs. The idea is to keep the affirmation at the fore in my mind and to repeatedly direct my to-do list foreman to create the new view of the world that I live in. (Like looking for the red-and-white truck.) I let the affirmation move around and mellow (as in removing the model year in the Studebaker Hawk example).

Here's an example of evolving and mellowing:

I weigh 168 pounds
To … I weigh less today than yesterday.
To … I am a good weight for my lifestyle and feel great all the time.
To … I look good in my clothes – out of them too ❀.
To … I have a healthy body and carry myself proudly.
To … I am vigorous and like to get involved.
To … I shine, I rule, I smile, I go, go, go; life is wonderful.
To … I am lean and able.
To … I eat and exercise to the betterment of my healthy body.

And so on. The subconscious is going to have a tough time ignoring all of these directives to get me to where I want to go. Notice how the statements quickly got to the real issues and it wasn't the weight per se. Note also the inclusion of emotion and action words. Imagine standing and walking differently after writing these. By bringing the issue to the conscious each day, the mind is bound to do something about it. If I have all these things already, my mind watches to make sure I keep them. If I don't have them, it sets to work to go and get them.

Shakti Gawain in *Creative Visualization* recommends ending written affirmations with the following:

> This, or something better, is now manifesting itself for me, harmoniously and satisfactorily, for the higher good of all concerned.

The inclusion of "or something better" reminds us that we tend to ask from a paradigm of finiteness. The subconscious (the universe) is an expression of the infinite and must therefore, logically, also be infinite. Including "or something better" removes some of the self-imposed boundaries that our minds can put on either the thing we want, how we believe we will achieve it, or both. Keeping my affirmations at the results level (the what) is also reinforced using Gawain's phrase.

The other part that I personally appreciate is "for the highest good of all concerned." This acknowledges that we are interrelated beings and again underlines the abundance of the universe. I can indeed have anything and receive it without denying someone else anything at all.

When an Affirmation Is Not Working

Following are a few hiccups that some people encounter.

1. We sometimes believe that we are like cakes already baked – fully formed and unable to change. We are not cakes.

   My Self, as I have created me, just happens to be my present state, generated by all my prior affirmations. One child is interviewed in prison and explains that it was their parents who influenced them to be the way they now are. A sibling twin, who is a successful contributor to society, uses the same words. These two people experienced the same parents.

   I acknowledge the siblings were influenced by a million or more factors. Yet, I assert that both "cakes" were made as they presently appear to be through prior personal affirmation. I further assert that either, or both, of these cakes can be changed into any new cake that they desire to be.

If a person believes they are a final cake, unable to change, that in itself is the affirmation and it becomes their truth.

So, do I believe that I am a cake, finally baked and fully formed?

2. Another area in which an affirmation may falter is in affirming something that, down deep, my heart is not in. An example is an affirmation about my weight. I can affirm that "I weigh 168 pounds" or I can affirm, "I remain lean, vigorous and able physically, enjoying regular exercise and often working outdoors." The first one is specific, but the second one may be where my heart is. One thing about the more specific example is that I feel almost compelled to go looking for a scale to weigh myself. And what if I weigh 167 or 169 or any weight other than 168? One conclusion could be that I, or my affirmation, has failed, even though I may be meeting all the criteria of the second affirmation. So what does exact poundage matter? A further result can be disbelief that affirming is indeed the way that we create our respective worlds – even though this negative affirmation about the working of affirmations was accomplished instantly! Think on that one a minute.

3. Affirming someone else's version of what I want is unlikely to be a positive experience. If I do not want it or do not believe it is realistic, well, it simply goes nowhere. In the epilogue of the August 2002 issue of O *The Oprah Magazine,* Oprah explains how she fought with her body until she started to love and accept it and to affirm her

appreciation for what the body does for her. Her affirmations up until then had been someone else's "should" about her body. Makes so much sense.

4. Affirmations require patience. If I affirm a behavioral change, it takes time more than effort. Affirming is a natural process. When nature moves too fast in making a change we call it a disaster (earthquake). I allow myself to fill out the new version of me in a reasonable time. I can start to practice some parts of the new me right away, but maybe not all parts. The rewriting method really helps to sift "the new" into place.

5. The effort that may be needed to handle reactions to the new me can be significant and cause me to doubt. The reactions of others to the changed me are a vital component to the success of my affirming process. When I change, some others will subconsciously want to change me back so that they don't have to change themselves. Gee, didn't think my changing would involve so many others. Well it does, because all those others are attached to the "me" that they knew and had developed preferred methods of interaction with. My change is not necessarily comfortable for others. I need to recognize the negative reaction as a positive sign that my change is a good thing. Now I have more to give the world, even to the temporarily upset people.

   I smile. I say, "Thanks for noticing," "Yes, I have decided to make a little change," or, "Yup, I think I am done with that way of doing things," or, "I know, I am making things a little better for myself, and that old way of ____ is no longer serving me." I say, "Indeed I am and it feels great, thank you."

I need to experience affirmations in low gear before I hit the freeways. I need to gain confidence, build up a personal repertoire of examples that have done the job and to understand why. I need to explore examples that have not done what I thought they would and understand what they in fact did and why.

I am gentle with myself.

Boundaries – Further Exploration of "My Place"

Nathaniel Branden *(The Six Pillars of Self-Esteem)* partitions self-esteem into two main components, self-efficacy and self-respect:

Self-efficacy – confidence in the functioning of my mind, in my ability to think, understand, learn, choose, and make decisions; confidence in my ability to understand the facts of reality that fall within the sphere of my interests and needs; self-trust; self-reliance.

Self-respect – assurance of my value; an affirmative attitude toward my right to live and to be happy; comfort in appropriately asserting my thoughts, wants and needs; the feeling that joy and fulfillment are my natural birthright.

I have certain levels of self-efficacy and self-respect. While they describe positive aspects of myself, they are also boundaries, maximums. Any affirmation that I make needs to be consistent with my own perceived levels. "I know my place." If I wish to affirm my way to a more satisfying place, I need to begin with affirmations to expand the boundaries on my self-efficacy and self-respect, to enlarge "my place."

I search for "my place" first by looking at the present situation and then moving the picture to where I believe I want it to go. Once there, I check my feelings to test if this future place is still within "my place." If not, I look for the incongruity and again note the feeling. By progressively uncovering what about the desired new place is not yet comfortable I begin to learn about it, and in so doing demystify it. It begins to become familiar, if ever so slightly. By repeatedly revisiting and exploring I find myself adjusting, becoming comfortable, accepting each little part, much like attending fittings for a new outfit tailored just for me. Soon enough, the "new place" is formed in my mind in a way that I can include it in "my place." It may be that I found a previously unused or unacknowledged path from the former "place." It may be that I have found a way (and also allowed myself) to enlarge "my place" to include the new.

I could call this expanding my view of the world, stretching my comfort zone or widening my horizons. Without it my affirmations are restricted to my present view, present comfort zone, present horizon. If I am going to build a bigger house, I may need to get a bigger lot to put it on. Branden recommends the use of unfinished sentence stubs to uncover and dissolve our self-imposed limits. See "Sentence Stubbing" (page142).

In a way that comes naturally for me, I explore the reality of "my place" as it exists today. I go there. I write about it. I talk about it. I explore it thoroughly and repeatedly. I put my curiosity at the boundaries. I discover my personal limits, as I perceive them, and come to understand them, meaning that I challenge why the limits are where they seem to be. Use of the sentence stub here both uncovers the self-imposed boundary and moves it out further in a process that is really not work at all.

Who put a boundary there and what purpose does it serve?

Am I one who believes that riches are not within my reality? If so, is it possibly because of the Bible passage that says it is "easier for a camel to pass through the eye of a needle than for a rich man to enter the kingdom of heaven"? Is it possibly because my parents were working class immigrants? Is it because I don't believe I could fit in among people who are well off financially? What else?

If someone else positioned the boundary, why am I buying into it? And if I put it there, what do I need to do in order to just move it? Is this a permission issue?

Here we are at the heart of it all. Remove the boundary and the larger, better, bigger affirmation is already manifesting itself. Define the boundary and the boundary is already in question. Having been questioned, it is moved to give "my place" more room.

The Present Moment

The authority figures in our lives ask us what we will be when we grow up and can react to our answers with encouragement or ridicule. How we understand their answer is a major factor in what we indeed become.

We get a lot of our ideas from models, real (Uncle Bill) or imaginary (heroes on TV and in stories). When models are strong for us we gravitate toward emulating them. If our model is one who is less than we could be in any way, we are likely to limit ourselves.

Our view of our world is polluted by *our interpretations* of past experiences. Yet this view (often independent of reality) is the main foundation upon which we create our new expectations.

We have a great need to "fit in" and to get the "right answer." An artist taking a class out to paint a cityscape from across the river on a misty morning, asks, "What color is the water tank, the bridge and that apartment building?" The students dutifully answer, "White and green and brick red." Asked to look again at the objects through a card with a narrow slot in it, they come to realize that indeed the objects are all variations on blue-gray because of the mist and the low light of early morning. Why did they answer otherwise before?

Until the students can see truly (and therefore differently from perceptions about getting it right) and see only from the perspective of the "present moment," the students don't see at all. They instead simply regurgitate the "right answer" from a previous memory, wrong color and all.

To be blind to the truth of the present moment is an act of the ego and will often hurt us. Bonnie Prince Charlie of Scotland went forward to Culloden, out-gunned, outnumbered, and chose a field disadvantageous to the kind of fighting with which his remaining dispirited troops might have had any chance of success. He was not seeing what was before him. They were quickly decimated.

The present moment is timeless and therefore tireless. It is separate from the remorse of things past and thus the fear of things to come. I am free to choose my response to each and every situation that presents itself, and do so without any prejudice or any kind of habitual response, rather with fresh objectivity and complete open curiosity. The present moment is indeed the ultimate in freedom.

How powerful I am when in the present moment! This does not mean forgetting everything I ever knew and starting again with zero knowledge. Not at all. But it does mean "because we've always done it that way" is a phrase that I no longer use. It does mean meeting each person with acceptance and a positive expectation, rather than prejudgment.

How much more will others do for one who approaches them afresh in this open way? How does it feel to be met by someone who has no prejudice or lack of confidence in me, whose only expectation is that whatever I do will be perfect? How do I get into this magic headspace?

From a cold start, with a few decades of habit to unlearn, it might take a bit of effort. I get there one moment at a time. Moves toward present-moment living are understandably tentative at first. Once tried, however, the rewards are enough to provide the needed encouragement to try again.

There is nothing to control while in the present moment. Therefore, there is no pressure, no performance anxiety. I am open to those I encounter both in my acceptance of them as whole and in not wanting of myself either. When I am in this state of not judging myself, I am most powerful. Since I do not need to hide my insecurities or safeguard my path to future perceived dangers, I can simply do what is right in the now. Wow!

When I am in the present moment it is possible for others to be teachers for me. If I discount or categorize others through any kind of advance judgment, I block, at least partially, what they show me in word or action because of my judgment filter. I deny myself the opportunity to be openly curious and do not have eyes to see or ears to hear what others have to share. I am less than I could be and they sense my closedness and are, too, denied the possibility of being all that they can be – a lose-lose situation for sure.

Strengthening and Maturing Affirmations

Without looking back at the set of personal affirmations that I have already written, I do the following over the next ten days:

1. Rewrite the whole shebang, as I feel the memory of what I wrote, never minding the exact words; there is no concern about missing some, or of adding new ones.

2. Write just the word following each "I am."

3. Write just the verbs, the action words, movement, kapowwwww, zoom, whoopee.

4. Write a one-sentence summary of it all.

5. Write one word that represents the whole thing.

6. Write a new word that represents the whole thing.

7. Rewrite the whole works, allowing new expressions to flow onto the paper as they come to me. Let this one go on and on for pages and pages.

8. Since I am human, it took me seven days to create my new world, where it took God only six. But now I may rest. I do nothing today.

9. Day off again, since I am human and seem to believe that creating is hard work.

10. I compare the newly written version to the affirmations I had before starting this latest work. Now I write a fresh version of my personal affirmations about what, and how, I truly am in the world.

Sentence Stubbing

Another rather excellent method to effect changes within ourselves is sentence stub completion. I have seen this tool used in many books, but the best treatment I have experienced is by Nathaniel Branden in his exceptional book *The Six Pillars of Self-Esteem.*

One form of the sentence stub is:

> If I really wanted to increase ____ by 5 percent, I might …
>
> or
>
> If I really decided to increase ____ by 5 percent, I could …

The way these little gems work is that I complete the stub at least six, but not more than ten, times each morning, in writing. I let the sentence completions that come to mind, even a seemingly silly one, be the ones that I write down.

In the evening I complete a complementary stub, such as:

> When I bring 5 percent more conscious effort to
> ____ I ____ ...

This complement often engenders a "way of being" response, such as "... I am more patient" or "... I feel energized." Any completion is just perfect.

Do it for a whole week, morning and evening, without looking back at the ones written before. It doesn't matter if the completions that I am using today sound like the ones from other days. No matter. I go on with my day. I don't even think about the stubs for that day. On the weekend, I haul out all five of the completion sets from the prior week and read them. Then I immediately complete the following:

> If any of what I have written is true, it might be
> helpful if I ____ ...

I complete it once or as many times as I feel the resolve to actually do what the completion states. I set myself up for success. One is perfect. Two is equally perfect – if I will do what I say I will do. Maybe it feels good to write a handful and then just pick the one or two that I want to commit to. A-OK.

A few points:

- The use of "if" to start the sentence is essential because it allows the mind to play and tends to remove the "ya buts" that our logical mind puts up to stop so many new ideas.

- The use of "only 5 percent" of change in the area of interest also allows the mind to not get too concerned because it feels like only a little bit, again suppressing the "ya buts."

- The use of the “could” or “might” in the sentence reinforces that this is only conjecture and we don’t need to “ya but” the idea. It is safe to play.

- Including the “really” in the start of the stub lends some seriousness to the play and engages our competitive side, giving rise to more useful completions.

- Write the answers. Speaking will have some effect but writing more thoroughly engages the mind and the results are truly better because the completion is more deeply ingrained. Don’t skimp on this part. The written sentences are needed for the weekend part.

- Not looking at the old sentence stubs keeps the mind free to play afresh each day.

- Little things are perfect; it is after all only a 5 percent improvement. So chill on the Olympian effort. Relax, and just think of little increments because they are truly easy.

- Note the tone of the concluding stub. It encourages commitment because it gently suggests “I will.” And the resulting resolve is usually surprisingly strong. Even without doing the weekend part, the stub technique will generate positive change with no other effort other than doing the stub completions. Doing the weekend stub increases clarity and speeds things up. If you want to go faster, do the weekend stub too.

- Finally, I don’t recommend one do the stubs endlessly. A few weeks is an excellent period of time. Rest and do another one after a week or two off.

- Some may soon automatically use the technique in how they approach issues day to day, using a stub completion to solve a problem as it arises. That is very powerful:

  If I really wanted to have a workspace that is 5 percent cleaner, I might ____ …

  If I really wanted to spend 5 percent less of my time looking all over for tools, I could right now ____ …

  If I really wanted to reduce the reworks on these manufactured items by another 5 percent, I could right now ____ …

  If I really decided to improve my relationship with xxxx by 5 percent, I could ____ …

  If I really decided to give 5 percent more attention to strengthening my life partnership, I could ____ …

  If I applied 5 percent more energy to being self-aware, I could ____ …

  If I really decided to have more friends, I could ____ …

Notice the call to action in some of these last examples with the addition of "right now." That optional addition is a useful variation. The last one is also interesting. No 5 percent. Yet, as I read it, did I not have a useful completion come to mind? So it can work that way too.

Want to help your children deal with situations? Talk to them in stubs when they come to you with a problem and show them ways to complete the stub and ultimately get them to do some to demonstrate how capable they actually are (but maybe just don't know it).

Sentence stubbing develops the solution-seeking reflex, increases self-confidence, engenders an awareness of greater freedom.

Journaling

The conscious mind tends to give high priority to fitting in (on the advice of the gremlin/ego). That means the thoughts that are at the ready, at the fore of the mind, tend to be the ones that we are "supposed to" think. These are the expected, but not necessarily the true expressions, of my Self. These expressions don't question or push at my boundaries.

Journaling in a free-association fashion helps clear away the "supposed to" and uncover the truth as I now know it. One way to do this is to just let those top thoughts float off, allowing the more personal and real thoughts from the subconscious to percolate up.

To use the percolator, I fill it with water and above the water line I place the coffee grounds in a basket. Snap on the lid, with its little glass bubble in the top, and plug in the pot. At first not much seems to be happening. The water is heating, but I neither see nor hear anything. At some point, I hear a *glub* or a *shaaaa* and then silence again. A little while later, another *glub* and maybe even a burst of water, a bubble, shows in the glass top. And in not much more time the glass top is showing bubble after bubble as the water is now boiling and the percolator is beginning, at long last, to percolate the water through the coffee grounds. We don't have coffee yet. Now that the percolation is started, we can say with some confidence that in so many minutes (depending on how strong I like my coffee) the hot drink will be ready.

So, too, with the process of free-association journaling. I can start to write about my chosen topic and, well, nothing seems to be happening. The process requires my willingness to let nature take me where I am intended to go, even if it surprises or upsets. Writing in a free-association mode is difficult for those who are used to structure. Waiting for the coffee is very tough for those who are used to quick results. Journaling is most successful when I let the thoughts write themselves as they come and neither judge them nor bend them to a preconceived end. The bending is what my conscious mind is likely to do automatically, and that is what I am trying to get past in journaling. I sort of empty my conscious mind.

Why? So that I can tap into the answers to my questions without any bending by the automatic "shoulds" I carry around with me. I am no longer in an automatic mode, but have a fresh and open curiosity, from a present-moment stance. It is from the stance of the present moment that I see most truly, without the judgment of past experience and without the fear and planned protection about the future.

I just write. I don't review prior days' notes. I allow surprises to pass and keep on writing. The surprise was merely that first bubble in the top of the percolator. I let it flow. I am a passenger. The writing is the vehicle. The subconscious is the fuel. This experience is about self-discovery and peacefulness.

Stuck for what to write? Write, "I am stuck for what to write," and just follow the thoughts from there. The mind is never quiet for long. I follow my thoughts onto the paper.

How long does it take to get the full benefits of journaling? My personal experience is that it is unending in the levels of inspiration available. Whatever it gave before, it always seems to give more when done again. I can try it and see if I like it. Thirty days of twenty minutes a day would be a good trial period.

I Feel When Because And ...

Sometimes I just want to be heard in order to express a feeling. Something has happened or been happening and it is under my skin. If I just push it down and don't tell anyone, it will come back to the surface when I least expect it and bite me, and probably someone else too. And I will find myself living with an area of life that pushes me off my Natural Edge when I approach it again.

Imagine a situation where I am invited to help someone in another company develop a plan for a specific product introduction. We work for about two months and it is a good piece of work. The boss is kept informed and seems not just pleased but excited. Then imagine that I attend a meeting where this and other initiatives of that company are to be addressed. Out of the blue, the boss cuts the product initiative to zero, to the absolute astonishment of myself and my collaborator. I ask why and am told to be quiet, the decision is his and it is made. I am floored.

In order to deal with this productively I need to clear my emotions. Let's say that takes two days. Only then do I sit down to write the following. This is a situation where the "I Feel When Because And ..." formula is perfect.

Notes for My Talk with "the Boss"

> I am not satisfied with how our last interaction in the boardroom went because I think it may have damaged our relationship, which I value. I would like you to hear how I feel about it all.
>
> What I have to say has nothing to do with you. It has everything to do with how I am feeling and therefore it is totally my own responsibility. All I ask

of you is to allow me to say my piece. That would be very helpful to me and I would appreciate it.

My comments have to do with my reactions to our last interchange. I then want to offer a suggestion for our future interactions.

May I please tell you how I feel? OK?

Thank you for listening.

I felt surprised, confused, attacked, blindsided, scared, sad, cornered, dismissed, abused and not at all valued

When you simply stopped any discussion on the product introduction without any prior discussion or providing a reason other than that you had so decided.

Because I had carefully considered the results provided and thought them to be more than important, in fact vital, to the progress of John's work for you (John is the person I was asked to help).

...I then thought it would be no use to put my all into anything for you again, which ... was as far from satisfied with the results of my work as I have been in many years.

My ego was bruised.

And I want to interact with you in a way that compliments you and that compliments me, too. I sincerely request that we together find a way to insure that the sequence that occurred last time is never repeated.

Thanks for listening.

Delivering the "I Feel When Because And ..." is meant to clear me totally. I do it in order to become at peace with myself and with "the boss" (in this case), regardless of his reaction. What he did with the message I delivered would have nothing to do with me. I was done. I was clear.

This example is derived from a personal experience and from my notes on it. The result was that I did indeed feel cleared.

A few very important points need to be made here:

- First, obtaining permission from the person I wish to address is not optional. Without permission to tell someone how I feel, to then do so is an infringement and they have the right to leave in the middle of it.

- Second, I must be clear of emotion *before* I develop the statement. If I make the statement too soon, I am likely to lace it with innuendo and accusation that will not clear me but will inflame the situation.

- Third, I must be totally honest with myself both about the range of feelings I experienced and my true motivations around the whole matter. For instance, I admitted that I reacted from a bruised ego.

- Fourth, string the feelings list until I have to squeeze one more out. That last one is usually the closest to the real thing that is bothering me and it may not be lovely. I need to get it out or I am wasting my time. If I get it out I've learned something about myself.

- Last is to finish with a heartfelt statement about the future and to insure that the listener knows they can just walk away if they want/need to. Leave it in a place that allows me to truly call it done.

When I ask someone to listen to how I feel and ask permission, well, wow, what can they say? I have their attention. When I, in advance, let that someone off the hook for how I feel, well, they can stay unhooked and maybe even hear what I say and possibly learn something about me and about how we interact. When I require nothing more from that someone than to listen, they can usually do that. It allows them to control their involvement rather than rally to defend themselves.

To deliver a properly developed "I Feel When Because And ..." is an effort that benefits the author of it and probably the one who listens as well. If their permission is withheld, I am already clear anyway, having gone through the development of my true statements. The other person doesn't have to do a thing, and I am still clear.

Use with care and use with genuineness. It is a powerful formula. I have used it quite a few times and always found it bettered the situation.

Lots of variations are equally valid. Such as, "*When* you abcd, *I felt* xyz *because* defg *and* it would really be helpful to me if you would please ghij." That rolls off the tongue in a professional or personal situation where expressing how I feel has been allowed and is an established behavior. Go for it.

There are a number of books that develop these kinds of communication statements. They don't all call them "I Feel When Because And ..." but come very close to recommending that formula. One such book is *People Skills* by Robert Bolton, PH.D. He calls these "three-part assertion messages."

Here's an example from that book:

When you use my car and don't refill the gas
I feel unfairly treated
Because I then have to pay money for gasoline that I don't use.

The idea is basically the same. The one part that I really want to stress again is the long list of feelings. "I feel unfairly treated" is an absolutely valid and likely feeling in the above example, but is that all of it? Am I being completely honest with myself and am I getting myself cleared of all the emotion around this event? I assert that there is almost always more to it and that not until I run through the string to get to admitting what is really burning me up, can I get clear. Try it and decide for yourself.

When you don't take accurate phone messages
I feel ...
Because ...
And it would really help me out if you were
more careful and thorough in taking telephone
messages.
Thank you for listening.

The Failure Continuum

Did Tiger Woods always play golf the way he does now? If he played less well early on, was he a failure then and only a success later? Is a person "more" when they are five feet tall compared to when they were only four feet tall? And if so, are they failures when four feet tall? However well I do something today is it possible that I could do better tomorrow? Then am I a failure today? Am I a failure forever because I can always improve? What is our obsession with labeling ourselves as failures all about?

When we learned to walk, the atmosphere was one of, "Oh my, see how well you are doing. We are so proud of you! Come on you can do it, come to Mommy." If we accept that some children will walk earlier than others and not call any of them failures, why can't we apply the same sanity to adults, especially to ourselves? We have such an obsession with negatively judging that we have taken a word from another language that meant "to miss the center mark when shooting an arrow" and distorted it to mean a failure that only God can forgive – sin.

Without so-called failure, we have a much tougher road to learning, because we learn a great deal through the experience of contrast. When I try and don't get the result I want, I have far more information than I had going in. Failure is an essential tool for learning.

Maybe it is time that I let myself be myself and just go with the flow that suits me, sins and all. Maybe it is time to allow myself to be human.

We normally live in an endless stream of failures because we constantly raise the bar. No one fails if we set the bar low enough, but there is no satisfaction in a bar set so low. The rush, the meaning and fulfillment come from clearing the bar and willingly, even eagerly, raising it to grow again. "Sin" is just the path, a natural learning aid. The failure continuum is the proper place of wholeness for we who are on the human journey. Enjoy it.

When I first wrote this section I asked my daughter (twenty-eight years younger) to comment from her point of view. Here are her notes.

> How many arrows must we shoot before we hit the target? This brings to mind sayings such as "Practice makes perfect" and "If at first you don't succeed, try, try again." I would go so far as to change the last one to "If at first you don't succeed, do and do again." This comes from my belief that Yoda, when he said, "Do or do not – there is no try," was actually saying that trying is not positive enough, not strong enough a word. Yoda was thinking of Nike's slogan – "Just do it!" To do something, I think, means there is no failure. Whether or not things turned out as planned, you still did it. Take an actor in a show for instance. Say the critics hated the actor, but the actor personally took some risks and "did" it as best they could. That to me means success, not failure. To do something is to move forward, and moving forward, whether you are Tiger Woods practicing those shots or Luke Skywalker training with Yoda, moving forward always leads to success, never failure.

I think that being accepted is where "Practice makes perfect" comes in and also in how we measure success and failure. Everyone will have their own pace and will also have their own success and failure rating systems. Look at my experience of taking dance class at university. There were many people who were, I would say, more technically able or better dancers. Yet, that is one of the classes in which I experienced the most personal success. If I were to measure myself, and my performance, in that class against someone like Sherisse, who is a very good dancer, I might have said, "Boy, I failed that class. I can't dance half as well as Sherisse." But I looked at myself at the end of that class and said, "I can dance so much better than I could at the beginning. I can do double the moves I could do before."

As long as I keep moving forward on my own path and not on someone else's (e.g., Sherisse's), there will always be doing and, therefore, never failure. I don't even want to say that failure exists, but if we were to assume it does, I would say that the only real failure is to do nothing.

Enjoy your path in particular because everyone's is unique, everyone's is moving forward at a different speed, level and momentum. In Theatresports they always say that this is a good place to fail – "It's OK to fail here." I know what they are saying. They are trying to make us feel safe because so many people are afraid of failing. If they know it's safe to do so, they will go for it. I think it would be cool if that could be reworded as, "This is a great place to try everything, do anything and find out what works and what

> doesn't work. Keep what you like and throw away the rest." These are both basically saying that "sins" are a good thing because they allow us to move forward, and in moving forward we succeed or grow or find out what works.
>
> Sins, missing the bull's-eye on that target, are just measurements, really, of trying or doing again and again. They sound like good things to me.
>
> —Leslie Seiler

Rumi, the thirteenth-century poet and prophet, says it this way:

> Out beyond ideas of wrongdoing and rightdoing,
> there is a field.
> I'll meet you there.

- After Fred Astaire's first screen test, the memo from the testing director of MGM, dated 1933, read, "Can't act! Slightly bald! Can dance a little!" Astaire kept that memo over the fireplace in his Beverly Hills home.

- The parents of opera singer Enrico Caruso wanted him to be an engineer. His teacher said he had no voice and couldn't sing.

- A newspaper editor fired Walt Disney for lack of ideas.

- Louis Pasteur was only a mediocre pupil in undergraduate studies and ranked fifteenth among twenty-two chemistry students.

EPILOGUE

Somewhere along the way to here, something has touched home. I have brought my Self a little further out into the light of day. I am more.

One of the beautiful things about this journey is that there is always more. Not to undermine the growth I have felt to date, but to encourage me to keep on growing. Growth is an act of nature. Natural growth is easy and happens with gentle watering and fertilization and a daily connection to the sun. My growth is easy and happens with gentle encouragement and introspection (sometimes challenging introspection) and daily connection to love of my Self.

What are the parts of this book that have worked for me? I practice those and make them into habits.

What are the parts that maybe didn't quite work for me, yet are somehow still attractive/intriguing to me? I revisit those and, over time, let them talk to me.

What are the parts that resonate most strongly with my Self? I share those understandings with others because these are indicators of who and what I am.

Ultimately, what am I? What am I here for? What am I meant to do here? What is my contribution to the earth experience?

These questions, once answered, place me at my Natural Edge. What is the impact that I have on the world when I am at my Natural Edge?

- I am the virus that infects the world with Acceptance! —Joseph Seiler
- I am the gentle breeze that renews and freshens the spirit of the world! —Barbara Seiler
- I am the beat that teaches the world nonconformity! —business leader
- I am the chandelier that shows truth to the world! —fellow writer
- I am the explorer who brings communion to the world! —actor/producer
- I am the Divine Light that shows the people of the world their own light! —fellow personal coach
- I am the warm backroom messenger who brings real hope to the world! —senior business partner
- I am the "holy shit" that awakens the world to its greatness! —teacher

I notice that I have an impact when I am centered and true to my Self. When I am in this place of clarity and peace …

I am the … who … to the world!

Namaste

SOURCES

The following is a list of books that I can directly point to as having influenced my growth to the point of having written this book. Of course hundreds of other books have, in some way, influenced me. But these below are top of mind today, and most are referenced in my text. The three that I have used material from directly are marked with an asterisk (*) and the required publishers' permissions are listed at the end of the bibliography.

I also post interesting books that I have read on my web site at www.yournaturaledge.com in the resource section. So welcome to that anytime.

Allen, James. *As a Man Thinketh.* Peter Pauper Press Inc., undated

Beck, Martha. *Finding Your Own North Star: Claiming the Life You Were Meant to Live*. Three Rivers Press, 2001

Bolton, Robert, PH.D. *People Skills*. Touchstone, 1986

*Branden, Nathaniel. *The Six Pillars of Self-Esteem*. Bantam, 1994

Carson, Richard D. *Taming Your Gremlin: a Guide to Enjoying Yourself*. Harper Collins Publishers, 1983

Covey, Stephen R. *The 7 Habits of Highly Effective People*. Simon and Schuster, 1989

Foundation For Inner Peace. *A Course In Miracles*. Penguin Books, 1975

Fritz, Robert. *The Path of Least Resistance*. A Fawcett Columbine Book published by Ballantine Books, 1984

Gawain, Shakti. *Living In The Light: a Guide to Personal and Planetary Transformation*. New World Library, 1986

Hill, Napoleon. *Think and Grow Rich*. Ballantine Books, 1983

Houdsen, Roger. *Ten Poems to Change Your Life*. Harmony Books, 2001

Klauser, Henriette Anne. *Write It Down, Make It Happen*. Simon and Schuster, 2001

McGraw, Phillip C., PH.D. *Life Strategies: Doing What Works, Doing What Matters*, Hyperion, 1999

Richardson, Cheryl. *Take Time for Your Life*. Broadway Books, 1998

*Sher, Barbara. *I Could Do Anything: If I Only Knew What It Was*. Dell Publishing, 1994

Sinetar, Marsha. *Elegant Choices, Healing Choices*. Paulist Press, 1988

Stone, Sidra and Hal. *Embracing Your Inner Critic: Turning Self Criticism Into a Creative Asset*. Harper Collins Publishers, 1993

Walsh, Roger, MD, PH.D. *Essential Spirituality*. John Wiley and Sons, 1999

*Whitworth, Kinsey-House, Sandahl. *Co-Active Coaching*. Davies-Black Publishing, 1998

Permissions requested and received:

For the question strings in "Values Exploration 1 – Question Strings," page 39, and "The Wheel of Life," page 82:

Modified and reproduced by special permission of the publisher, CPP Inc., Palo Alto, CA 94303, from *Co-Active Coaching* by Laura Whitworth, Henry Kinsey-House, Phil Sandahl. Copyright 1998 by Davies-Black Publishing, an imprint of CPP, Inc. All rights reserved. Further reproduction is prohibited without the Publisher's written consent.

For the definitions in "Boundaries – Further Exploration of My Self," page 137, and the sentence stubbing exercise, page 142:

From *The Six Pillars of Self-Esteem* by Nathaniel Branden, copyright 1994 by Nathaniel Branden. Used by permission of Bantam Books, a division of Random House, Inc.

For the worksheet in "Values Exploration 3 – Immutable Me":

From *I Could Do Anything – If I Only Knew What It Was* by Barbara Sher, copyright 1994 by Barbara Sher. Used by permission of Dell Publishing, a division of Random House, Inc.

NOTES